截拳道

JEET KUNE DO KICKBOXING

by Chris Kent & Tim Tackett

EMPIRE BOOK/AWP LLC
Los Angeles, CA.

DISCLAIMER

Please note that the author and publisher of this book are NOT RESPONSIBLE in any manner whatsoever for any injury that may result from practicing the techniques and/or following the instructions given within. Since the physical activities described herein may be too strenuous in nature for some readers to engage in safely, it is essential that a physician be consulted prior to training.

Revised Edition published in 2025 by AWP LLC/Empire Books. Copyright (c) 2025 by AWP LLC/Empire Books/Chris Kent/Tim Tackett.

All rights reserved. No part of this publication may be reproduced or utilized in any form or by any means, electronic or mechanical, including photo- copying, recording, or by any information storage and retrieval system, without prior written permission from AWP LLC/Empire Books.

Revised edition Library of Congress Catalog Number:
ISBN-13: 978-1-949753-92-9
25 24 23 22 21 20 19 18 17 16 15 14 13 12
Library of Congress Cataloging-in-Publication Data
Jeet Kune Do Kickboxing by Chris Kent and Tim Tackett -- ed. p. cm.
ISBN 978-1-949753-92-9 (pbk. : alk. paper) 1. Martial arts-- philosophy. 3. Large type books. I. Title. GV1124.3.F720
25437861.815'3--dc22
20620101924

Printed in the United States of America.

DEDICATION

This book is dedicated to the Creator, who is responsible for all life and knowledge—and to Daniel Inosanto, whose friendship, guidance and caring showed us that the martial arts, like life itself, is a process, not a product.

ACKNOWLEDGEMENT

To everyone who has contributed to our growth as individuals and as martial artists, there are far too many to name. Our thanks to you all.

CONTENTS

ABOUT THE AUTHORS 6
INTRODUCTION 10
HISTORY 12
BASIC HAND TOOL DEVELOPMENT 15
BASIC FOOT TOOL DEVELOPMENT 58
BASIC USE OF TRAINING EQUIPMET 83
ATTACK BY COMBINATION 89
PROGRESSIVE INDIRECT ATTACK 101
DEFENSIVE TOOLS AND DRILLS 107
ATTACK BY DRAWING 121
KICKBOXING TRAINING DRILLS 127
CONCLUSION 147
THE CONTINUING ALLURE OF JEET KUNE DO 148

ABOUT THE AUTHORS

CHRIS KENT

With over 50 years of experience, Chris Kent is widely acknowledged as one of the world's foremost authorities on Jeet Kune Do and has gained international recognition for his knowledge and leadership in perpetuating the art, training methods, and philosophy developed by the legendary Bruce Lee. Chris is considered one of the few individuals in the world having total comprehension of all facets of Lee's martial art.

In 1973, Chris became the youngest and final member admitted into Dan Inosanto's now fabled "Backyard JKD" group during Bruce Lee's lifetime. He studied with and assisted Inosanto for over 13 years, mastering his skills and traveling extensively both nationally and internationally while serving as Inosanto's personal assistant for seminars and public exhibitions. In 1982, Chris became one of the first students to be awarded the prestigious title of Full Instructor under Inosanto.

In the over five decades that he has been intimately involved in Jeet Kune Do, while holding true to the original spirit and vision with which Bruce Lee developed Jeet Kune Do, Kent has performed extensive research into the foundations of the art from a technical, philosophical, and spiritual perspective, as well as educating himself in the fields of exercise physiology, kinesiology, and human performance. This commitment to continuous improvement has made him one of the most sought-after instructors of Jeet Kune Do and its applications. As a teacher and professional consultant, Kent has traveled the world, teaching and sharing the benefit of his expertise in Jeet Kune Do with thousands of people.

Chris' friendship and affiliation with Lee's family, personal assistants, students, and friends allows him to hold a unique position in the JKD world – a direct pipeline to Bruce Lee's art and philosophy. According to Linda Lee Cadwell (Bruce Lee's wife) -- "I am in awe of the growth I have witnessed in my friend Chris Kent. I have known Chris for close to 50 years from the time he first took up the practice of Bruce Lee's way of martial arts, Jeet Kune Do. Chris not only learned the martial aspect of Bruce's teachings but also his methods of self-reflection as a goal to personal development".

Possessing an exuberant teaching style as well as an uncanny ability to transfer knowledge to students and teachers alike, Chris is a teacher par excellence, whose innovative teaching and training methods help students to maximize their physical skills and achieve their full potential as martial artists. As a teaching consultant, Chris shares his passion for Jeet Kune Do with other instructors, who, in turn, share the art and philosophy with their students, Chris has worked in a consultant capacity and collaborated with numerous JKD instructors and schools, assisting them regarding such things as training protocols, teaching methodology, and training curriculum design.

Recognized for his knowledge and expertise and known as a "teacher of teachers"; Chris' goal is to help develop instructors who are equally passionate about JKD, and who possess the ability to convey their knowledge to the highest degree through movement and language.

Driven by a passion and desire to share authentic knowledge and insights regarding Jeet Kune Do, Chris is an accomplished writer and author. In addition to the books he has authored/co-authored on Jeet Kune Do, he has both written and for and appeared in countless martial art publications both nationally and internationally, including Inside Kung Fu, Black Belt, Martial Arts Masters, Budo International, Combat, Martial Arts Illustrated, and Bruce Lee Mania. Seeking to share his knowledge in all forms of media Chris wrote and produced three series of training DVDs which remain the standard of the industry.

Chris is not only one of the world's foremost authorities and experts on Bruce Lee's martial art training process, but also on his philosophy of self- actualization and personal liberation. His recent book, "LIBERATE YOURSELF! – How to Think Like Bruce Lee" and its accompanying workbook detail how individuals can apply the philosophical tenets of self-actualization utilized by Bruce Lee to their own lives. As a consultant and personal development specialist, Chris has helped countless individuals including celebrities, professional athletes, and corporate executives achieve liberation of body, mind, and spirit so that they can attain their goals and live a rich and rewarding life.

An inspiring and effective communicator, Chris has been a featured guest speaker on numerous radio talk programs, podcasts, and at public events, discussing not only Bruce Lee and his art and philosophy of Jeet Kune Do, but also how the much broader application of the principles can enhance an individual's personal and professional life. In 2023 he was a featured speaker at TEDx Youngstown "Life Happens."

In addition to his expertise in Jeet Kune Do, Chris also holds the title of Full Instructor in the Filipino martial arts of Kali-Escrima under Inosanto; and in 1976 was awarded the title of "Escrimador". In 1988 Chris received a Moniteur certificate (Teaching credential), Silver Glove (Technical) and Bronze Glove (Competition) rankings in the French Kickboxing sport of Boxe Francaise-Savate from the French Federation.

As part of his belief in giving back to the community, Chris created "S.A.V.E." (Safety Against Violence Education) a personal safety awareness training program which teaches personal safety education and self-protection skills to women and children as well as businesses and corporations.

In 1996, Chris was a one of the co-founders of "The Bruce Lee Educational Foundation." For five years he served as a member of the Board of Directors, then moved to an advisory position to the re-established "Bruce Lee Foundation."

In Hollywood, Chris martial art skills led to stunt work, serving as a technical advisor and fight action choreographer for both television and feature films. "Miami Vice" creator/producer Anthony Yerkovich, "Pink Panther" film director/producer Blake Edwards, and The Incredible Hulk, Lou Ferrigno are among the elite Hollywood clientele who sought Mr. Kent out for his technical assistance and training expertise.

Working in the field of professional sports, Chris served as a training consultant to professional sports teams including the San Francisco 49ers. He has also worked with many law enforcement personnel and has been extensively involved in the field of executive security for the entertainment industry, including such events as The Golden Globe Awards and American Film Institute Special Tributes. For three years after its opening, Chris served as Director of Security for Santa Monica's "Buffalo Club", an exclusive, private supper-club catering to high-profile members of Hollywood's entertainment industry.

Social media platforms:

Website: https://ckjkd.com
Facebook: https://www.facebook.com/ckjkd
Pinterest: https://www.pinterest.com/jkd4life/
YouTube: https://www.youtube.com/@chriskentjeetkunedo123
https://www.youtube.com/@chriskentjkd_dpl
https://www.youtube.com/@ChrisKent-ThinkLikeBruceLee
Instagram: https://www.instagram.com/ck_jkd_dpl/

ABOUT THE AUTHORS

TIM TACKETT

While in the U.S.A.F., Sifu Tackett was stationed in Taiwan for almost three years. While he was there, he studied Kuo Shu (Kung Fu). His wife was working as a teacher at the Taipei American School during the day, and he was working in the evening at the Shu Lin Kuo Air Force Station. Since he had his days free, he started to look for something to occupy his time. One of his friends recommended that he take up martial arts. He ended up training six hours a day, six days a week. While in Taiwan, he studied two types of Hsing-I, Tai Chi, Northern and Southern Shaolin, White Crane, and Monkey Boxing. After his discharge from the Air Force, he continued working on his college degree. Since he had a wife and two children to support, he opened a full-time Kung Fu school in Redlands, California, while starting as a junior at the University of California, Riverside campus, in 1966.

In 1967, he saw Bruce Lee demonstrate JKD at Ed Parker's tournament in Long Beach, CA, and wanted to start studying with him right on the spot. However, he soon realized that he would not have enough time until after he finished college. In 1968, he started a Master of Fine Arts program at UCR and no longer had time to teach martial arts full-time. So he closed down his school and rented a hall in Redlands two nights a week, where he taught what he called "Chinese Karate," as hardly anyone had heard of "Kung Fu," let alone "Kuo Shu." In 1970, he received his M.F.A. and began teaching drama in high school. Soon after, his first student, Bob Chapman, and he, on the recommendation of Dan Lee, sought out Dan Inosanto. Dan had opened a backyard Jeet Kune Do school after Bruce Lee closed his Los Angeles Chinatown school shortly before moving to Hong Kong to star in movies. Both men felt privileged to be accepted into Dan Inosanto's backyard class. The class consisted of about 10 students, and Sifu Tackett got to meet for the first time such JKD luminaries as Bob Bremer, Dan Lee, Richard Bustillo, Jerry Poteet, and Pete Jacobs. Later, Chris Kent, Ted Lucaylucay, and Jeff Imada joined the private group of students.

In 1973, Dan Inosanto honored Tackett with the rank of "Senior First," and he was given permission to have a small Jeet Kune Do group. In Dan's backyard school, it was always stressed that JKD was something special. There were certain techniques that Bruce Lee did not want given out outside of what we all felt was a small and special group. Dan told us that Bruce said, "If knowledge is power, then why pass it out indiscriminately?"

Like many Jeet Kune Do students, Tackett received supplemental training in Western boxing, Thai boxing, wrestling, and Wing Chun. He has been described by Dan Inosanto as "one of the most knowledgeable JKD instructors in the world."

Sifu Tackett taught the principles of JKD and used them as tools to examine the martial arts he had learned up to that point. He found that much of what he had been teaching previously was not very efficient. Since he didn't want to teach JKD openly, he closed the school and moved the senior group to his garage, where he started the famous "JKD Wed Night" group.

These are the three core concepts of the JKD Wednesday Night Group as described by Tim Tackett. *The Core Principle is "Maintaining and Utilizing Distance". "In order to do that one must be able to use distance for both attack and defense. Too many people prioritize one or the other and end up unbalanced. Instead, people should train as if they are both attacking and defending from the "Fighting Measure" using proper footwork."*

The first core principle is the "Leg Obstruction". "The primary defensive and offensive attack is the leg obstruction. Most of the time, you will be able to use the leg obstruction defensively. It is important to be able to use leg obstruction offensively as well as one may need to strike first. The main reason to practice the leg obstruction is to use it against an opponent that practices intercepting as their main defense. When attacking with the leg obstruction, you may enter based on the opponent's movement patterns or telegraphed strikes. From this point, you can trap or strike depending on the opponent's stance."

The second core principle is the "Finger Jab Drill". "This drill is one of the most important and foundational drills. Its goal is to reduce and eliminate the telegraphing of strikes. In this drill, one partner will stand with their hands raised to block the other partner's incoming finger jab. The partner jabbing should aim to touch the forehead of their partner without the partner parrying their strike. If the blocking partner is able to parry their strike, they should announce what prompted their parry so the partner can aim to eliminate the movement that caused them to block. It is essential to practice all drills with varying partners in groups of two to learn to adapt to different movement patterns. Both partners will benefit as the attacker eliminates the preparation and the parry partner will learn to notice preparation. Once you master this drill, you can hit without intention."

Finally the third core principle is the "Time Commitment Theory." "This was taken directly from Bruce Lee's notes and is one of the key teachings of our group. The theory states that any type of technique requires a certain amount of time. For example, a straight punch would include both the forward and backward motion of the punch as well as the recovery time to return to a proper stance. The more time a certain movement takes, the more vulnerable one is to counterattacks. One must weigh the options and make smart decisions with the "Time Commitment Theory" in mind. A combination of varying types of punches and kicks should be trained. The "Time Commitment Theory" is one of the best tools one has to analyze their techniques.

Social media platforms:

Website: https://jkdwednite.com
Facebook: https://www.facebook.com/TimTackettJKD
Instagram: www.instagram.com/jkdwng

INTRODUCTION

How did this book, "Jeet Kune Do Kickboxing" come into being? Tim and I had become friends since I began training in JKD under Dan Inosanto in his backyard gym in Carson, California in June,1973 (he was already training with Dan when I joined). In the mid-1980's several of us discussed the idea with Dan of writing some books about various facets of JKD, because at the time there so much misinformation concerning it floating around the marketplace. Dan was all for it and gave us the go-ahead. He also told us that we should feel free to use the name 'Jeet Kune Do' with the books as we were trained in it and aptly qualified to write about it. Larry Hartsell had also expressed interest in possibly writing books to share information with the public, so it was mutually agreed upon that we would write about different aspect of JKD so that no one would step on anybody else's toes and several books would not all come out covering the same thing. Tim and I decided to collaborate and co-write our first book about the kickboxing elements of JKD. Initially we talked about the idea of writing several books dealing with the kickboxing facet of JKD (however later decided to write "Jun Fan/Jeet Kune Do - The Textbook" in order to give people a clear overview about JKD and various training methods). Larry decided he would focus on the grappling element of JKD (In actuality, Tim co-wrote Larry Hartsell's grappling books with him, however due to issues with Black Belt Publications with whom Tim had written two books on Hsing-I kung fu, his name was left off them).

The Kickboxing Element of Jeet Kune Do

It's well-known that Bruce Lee was concerned with self-defense and real-world application of martial art techniques and strove to bring more realism to his training, which was done primarily through the practice of full-contact kickboxing sparring. Lee recognized that the only way he could truly know whether a technique worked or not in reality and under pressure was by taking it out onto the training floor and put it to the acid test of freelance sparring. So, he subjected all the techniques he encountered in his research to the "litmus test" of sparring to find out their efficiency and effectiveness in alive, stressful situations. Through sparring he was able to determine what worked and what didn't, what needed adjusting and refining, and what needed to be tossed out.

In addition, Lee recognized the mental qualities specific to fighting could only become evident in hard, full-contact sparring sessions. Only in a sparring experience could the individual develop to the highest degree the ability to compete to the best advantage against an opponent, to exhaust their strength and energy reserves with maximum economy and sense of purpose, and to "surpass themselves."

For these reasons Bruce Lee referred to sparring as the "lifeblood" of Jeet Kune Do and considered it the most vital ingredient and placed (it) at the top of the list of his martial art skill training. However, Lee also recognized that full-contact sparring, although an essential and very important part of his martial arts training and being prepared for a real fight, was just that, a part. It did not constitute the whole of training.
Sparring may reveal your strengths and weaknesses as a fighter, but you can't correct those things during sparring because you're in a stress situation and cannot stop the action. You can only work [on correcting] your flaws and developing your strengths after the sparring, in your self-training and with the use of what we refer to in JKD as 'alive' training drills and exercises.

Jeet Kune Do Kickboxing was originally written and published in 1986. Much has changed in the martial art world since that time. There have been advancements in such things as training methodology, equipment, nutrition, etc. Mixed martial arts as a combative sport exploded around the globe and countless 'hybrid' martial art systems have come into existence and now flourish. The undeniable fact is that many of these things can be directly attributed to Bruce Lee and his revolutionary approach to martial art training. Nevertheless, we feel this book will offer the reader a good view of what was happening up to that time with regard to the kickboxing element of Jeet Kune Do, how it fit into the overall structure of the art, and how we trained at the time, wearing shoes while working out, donning various types of protective gear when sparring, utilizing different tools at various times, and training on concrete floors. Included are such things as basic hand and foot tool development, use of various types of training equipment, examples of the five ways of attack, and basic kickboxing drills.

We enjoyed writing Jeet Kune Do Kickboxing and sharing insights into JKD training with others, and we hope you enjoy reading (or re-reading) it.

In the Spirit of JKD,

Chris Kent and Tim Tackett.

HISTORY

Bruce Lee's kickboxing phase began in 1965 when he moved to Los Angeles from Oakland to pursue his acting career. Prior to that time he was Jun Fan/Wing Chun oriented.

Dan Inosanto was among a small handful of students that Bruce taught privately in his living room between 1965 and 1966. In late '66, Bruce began to conduct small semi-public Gung-Fu classes behind Wayne Chan's Pharmacy in Los Angeles Chinatown. In 1967 the Chinatown school on College Street was opened. It was during this time that Bruce Lee's kickboxing era flourished.

The secret "closed-door sessions" were devoted to physical conditioning and tool development, utilizing all types of training equipment like focus gloves, heavy bags, top and bottom bags and football shields. *Everything* was contact oriented and sparring was the crucible, the ultimate testing ground that all the students had worked on in training. Basic trapping, sensitivity and various types of sparring were used (one on one, two vs. one, etc.) to develop timing and distance.

The arts influencing the kickboxing phase were diverse in structure and origin. Western boxing, Thai boxing, Savate, Northern and Southern Gung-Fu kicking, Sikaran, modified Wing Chun, among others, were used.

The use of body armor was used for safety during full contact sparring in the early days, but was gradually eliminated as the kickboxing progressed. No strict uniform dress code ever existed,

with students wearing anything they wanted, even construction boots.

In 1970, Dan Inosanto greatly influenced the curriculum by adding Filipino boxing (Panantukan). There were two reasons for the addition. First, it added more sophistication to the Western boxing and secondly, it added the ability to drill realistically and combatively without each student bashing the other's face in every workout. The Filipino training methods were developed from their stick-fighting methods to allow a student to "survive" in training.

Since then, many new training drills and methods were synthesized into the kickboxing curriculum. Like modern athletics, older methods are updated and changed where necessary, while fundamental principles remain. Students learn body mechanics and body motion and then "make it their own." What each individual chooses may be different—some favor hands over feet, some favor feet over hands, but they all learn to understand the strengths and weaknesses of each facet.

As in athletics, to comprehend what a martial artist does, to appreciate how he pursues his art, you must understand the art. You must speak the language. And the martial artist should be able to communicate effectively in his chosen medium of expression. That is why Jeet Kune Do has remained so long a mystery to so many people. It is one art, but expresses itself in many languages. It is a strangely complex and mystifying animal. What is attempted here is to de-mystify it a little.

Like any formidable opponent, the animal must become known before it can be challenged with any surety of success. To know it, you must study and observe it. Not for weeks or months, but every day for years. Even with knowledge and training more is required. Maturity and a deep comprehension of combative principles are necessary. The animal is cunning, continually changing, forever adapting.

What is so time-consuming is not so much the mastering of each of the individual elements involved, but understanding and embracing the total concept. To the unknowledgeable observer JKD may only appear to be various separate elements such as boxing, wrestling, Wing Chun, loosely strung together to create one generalized martial art. But that is an illusion, and to embrace the illusion is to invite defeat. It is a single entity, both an art and a science, and understanding that in all its ramifications is the key to successfully engaging and doing battle with the animal. It must be understood. It must dictate the plan for training, and permeate every hour of the martial artist's study.

The animal is a whole with many parts, commitment to any single portion of which will detract from the rest.

So how does one go about studying the animal? The same way one would approach any athletic endeavor. Combative situations combine different elements, and change from moment to moment. It may stress speed one moment, strength the next, then resilience, then endurance.

Every one of the combative skills has its own technique, its own motion that must be developed and perfected, the right move at the right time. In any physical movement there is always a most efficient and lively manner to carry it out, that is regarding leverage, balance, economical use of motion. It must be learned first, the same way one learns a lesson. But then it must be taken beyond that level. A martial artist thinks while learning, and that is how it should be. In an actual fight situation there will be little or no time for thoughts. By then each action must be second nature to the individual, the same way he brushes an annoying fly away from his face. This automaticity of response is what one seeks.

In a time of narrowing expertise and specialization, the JKD practitioner is the super all-rounder—a martial artist whose specialty is the overall picture. Such an accomplishment requires a tremendous commitment of energy and training.

The incredible diversity of combat means that JKD training is intentionally general in scope. Particular emphasis may be placed on different aspects at different times in order to increase a student's awareness in these various arenas. But the essence is to understand a particular art in order to be able to deal with it—not to become a 'boxer' or a 'wrestler'. It is to enter into their realm, experience it, but not be caught up in it. Unfortunately this is where a lot of people fall into a trap and start to think that "boxing is where it's at." It is 'a' truth, not 'the' truth. All arts have advantages and disadvantages, none possesses everything.

A JKD practitioner cannot study 10 times as hard or 10 times as long as a martial artist who specializes in one method. He must train 10 times as smart. The ultimate goal is to get as good as your genetic potential will allow in each of the elements—and to be able to shift from one to another without stopping the mind to think about it. And sparring is the testing ground for the street.

The animal is yourself. The essence is to be in command of your body, to make it do what you want it to do when you want it to do it. That's what JKD is about, and what makes it "uniquely complicated simplicity."

BASIC HAND TOOL DEVELOPMENT

To use an analogy related to warfare, in JKD we often refer to the legs as the heavy artillery and the arms as the infantry. In military tactics, when an army wishes to conquer a city, there are certain methods. You may stay outside the city all day long and shell it with heavy artillery. But, regardless of the damage you may inflict, in order to take the city, you must still go in with the infantry.

For this reason the development of one's punching tools is of paramount importance. There are many types of punches, all of which should be learned to be thrown from a variety of angles, and combined with footwork and body motion to make them more effective.

For instance, there are several types of lead jabs. Which one a fighter chooses to use is dependent upon the situation. The wider his punching arsenal is, the more choices he will have.

Some punches may be classified as minor blows in that, while they are not ordinarily designed to knock out an opponent, they aid in setting up a major or knockout blow.

Learn and practice punching with economy of motion, accuracy, and from a variety of angles, both singly and in combination.

WARNING: The authors and publisher are not responsible in any manner whatsoever for any injury which may occur by reading and/or following the instructions herein.

BASIC HAND TOOLS WITH EQUIPMENT

THE BASIC JKD STANCE (Bai Joing)

This stance is the basic JKD stance. Both feet are at approximately a 45-degree angle. The front foot is turned inwards to help protect the groin. The rear foot is at an angle to help (as we'll see later) the power of the punch. The rear heel is raised to help give a springing action to your footwork and to help make you a more elusive target. The toe of the front foot and the heel of your rear foot should be on the same line.

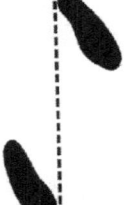

This offers maximum protection for your groin while still allowing you to kick with your rear foot without moving your front foot which is important for non-telegraphic movement.

Both knees should bend to add strength to your stance and flexibility and speed to your movements. The width of stance will vary according to individual preference keeping within the principles that the stance should not be too short to be weak or too long to be static or rigid. At the beginning level you should keep your weight approximately 50 percent on each leg.

The hand positions are not static but will vary from both hands held high to the front hand held low to protect the low line while the rear hand is high to protect the high line.

The important thing about the basic JKD stance is that it is never static. It is meant to be a stance you can deliver a powerful attack from while at the same time a stance that you can move from to avoid your opponent's attack.

From the basic stance you can:

Step to your right with your front foot.

Step to your left with your rear foot.

Step forward with your front foot while angling to the right.

Step forward with your rear foot while angling to the left.

All of the above pictures show the JKD stance with the right foot forward. Most right-handed JKD practitioners prefer the right lead for the following reasons.

1. Since the front hand is used for the stop hit (see below) it makes sense to have your most powerful hand forward.
2. Since the front leg is used for the stop kick (see below) the same reason applies.
3. Since your left hand is weaker it makes sense to carry farther back so it will have further to travel to the target and will gather more momentum which will give it more power.

The left-handed fighter will of course prefer the left lead. Many right-handed JKD fighters because of Western boxing training or personal preference will be more comfortable fighting mainly out of a left lead while many will shift from left to right lead.

Since an important JKD principle is whatever works for the individual, you should practice using both leads. While most of the techniques used in the book are done from the right lead, you should give equal time to working these techniques out of a left lead also. Then you can see what will work best for you in any given situation.

FRONT HAND TOOLS
FLICKER JAB

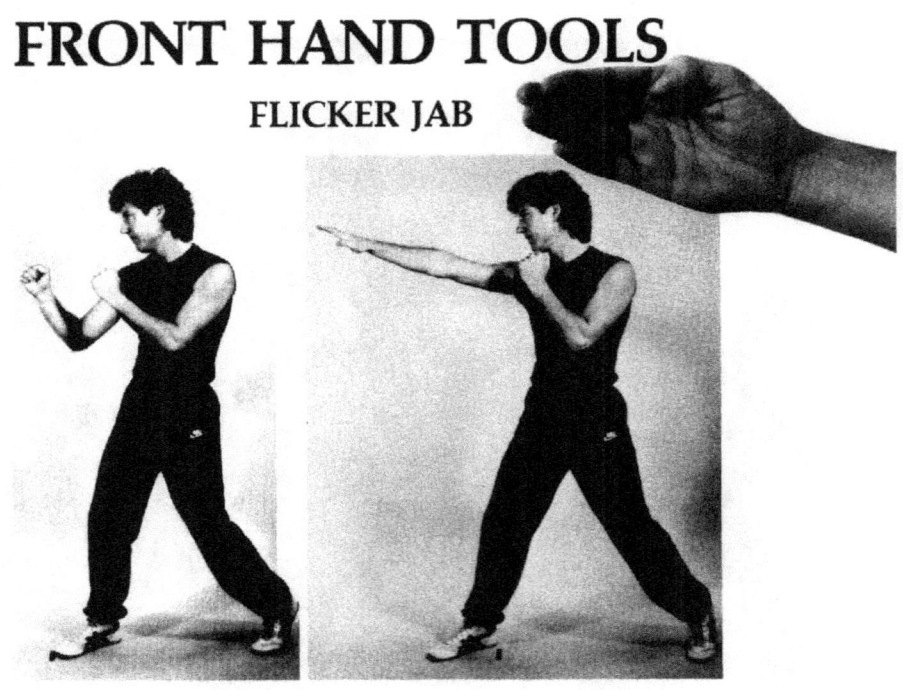

The flicker jab is the fastest jab. It is also the weakest jab. Since it is a weak jab it is usually used as a finger jab to the eyes. Since it is so fast and requires little energy, it is also used as a probe to test your opponent's defense or as a fake to set up an attack to another line.

To perform the flicker jab shoot your hand out from the elbow directly to your opponent's eyes while keeping as relaxed as possible. To gain a little more power transfer some of your weight to your front leg. As soon as you finish your flicker jab you should immediately follow with another attack or return to the on guard position.

Depending on distance, the flicker jab can be done from a stationary stance or you can take a slight step forward with your front foot.

THE SPEED JAB

The speed jab is a more powerful jab than the flicker jab. To perform the speed jab shoot your hand to the target by throwing your shoulder forward. You can do the speed jab from a stationary stance or by taking a short step forward with your front foot as pictured. The speed jab is usually used to keep your opponent off balance, to set up another technique, or to keep your opponent from moving toward you.

19

Any jab can be done from a low guard to a high guard position.

Speed jab from a high guard.

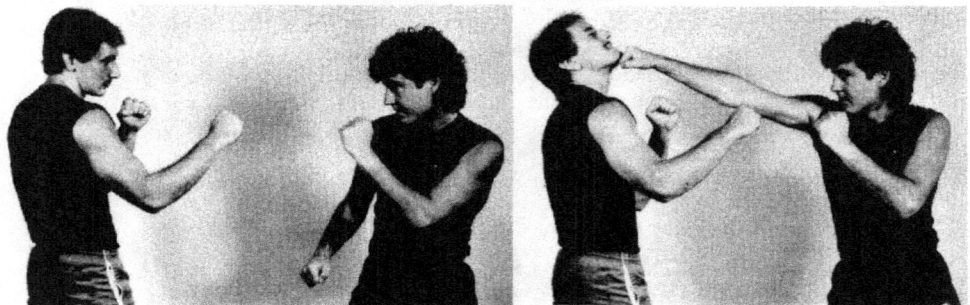

Speed jab from a low guard.

THE POWER JAB

The power jab is one of the most powerful of the front hand tools. The power jab starts with a powerful twist of your rear foot which transfers most of your weight to your front leg. Make sure your hip as well as your shoulder thrust forward. This can also be done from a stationary stance or you can step forward with your front foot as pictured. When you step forward make sure your rear foot pushes forward. If hitting with a horizontal fist, as pictured, twist your fist on impact, since it requires more energy to throw a power jab, and it takes more of a commitment. It takes longer to recover from throwing this type of jab. With this in mind, make sure you have a clear opening before throwing a power jab.

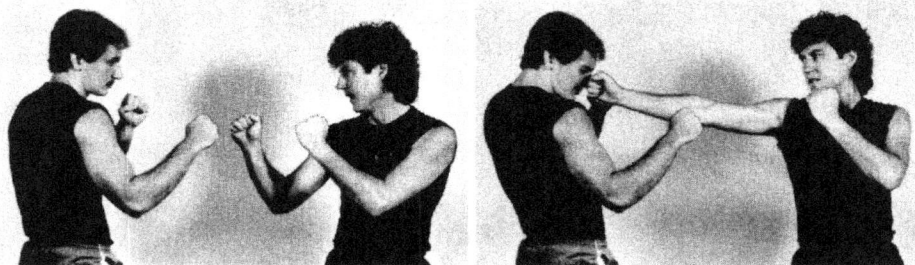

The power jab can also be done with a vertical fist to the nose like a Wing Chun punch.

THE ENTERING LEAD

The entering lead is used to bridge the gap, to move from kicking range to hand range. It is also used to enter to trapping or grappling range. You can do the entering lead with a flicker, speed, or power jab.

To do the entering lead push off hard with your rear foot as you step forward with your front foot. Your fist should make contact a split second before your foot hits the ground. The rear foot then slides forward. All of this is done in a split second.

THE DEFENSIVE JAB

As its name suggests the defensive jab is used to defend against an attack. As your opponent attempts to hit you with a hard attack, drop your weight back on to your rear leg as you jab with your front hand.

WHIPPING JAB

The whipping jab is performed much like the power jab. The main difference is that after you make contact with a power jab, your hand returns straight back to the on guard position, but as you make contact with the whipping jab your arm snaps to the inside.

While this snapping action will add a powerful momentum to your punch it will also leave you open to your opponent's rear hand. Make sure there is a target and that you can hit it before you attempt this punch.

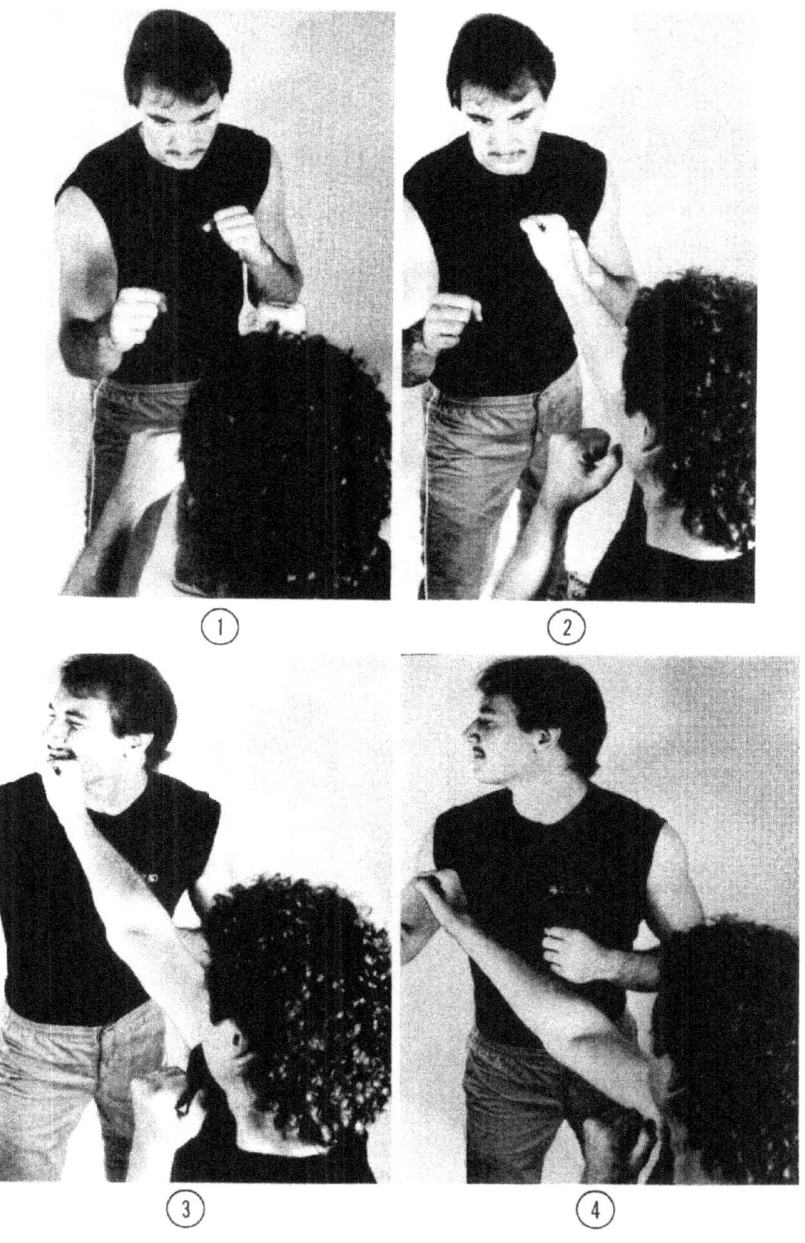

GENERAL JAB PRINCIPLES

1. Keep relaxed as you throw the jab. Try and keep the bicep relaxed.
2. Do not focus your punch, instead hit through your target.
3. Do not cock your fist back before you punch as this will telegraph the punch. Rather punch from where your hand is.
4. Make sure you cover your head with the rear hand.

Depending on your relationship to your opponent, your cover can be on the left side of your head.

Or the right side of your head.

5. Remember you can angle your body as you punch. You can do this as you slip a punch or to make yourself a more elusive target.

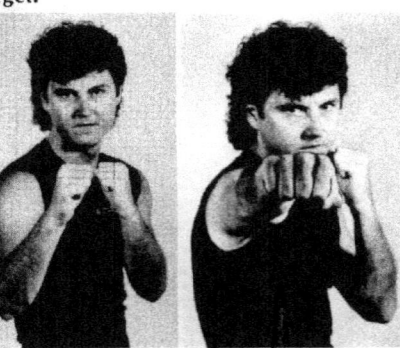

Straight

Angle to the right

Angle to the left

6. You can hit to the **inside** or the outside of your opponent's cover depending on how he covers.

Hitting on the inside line

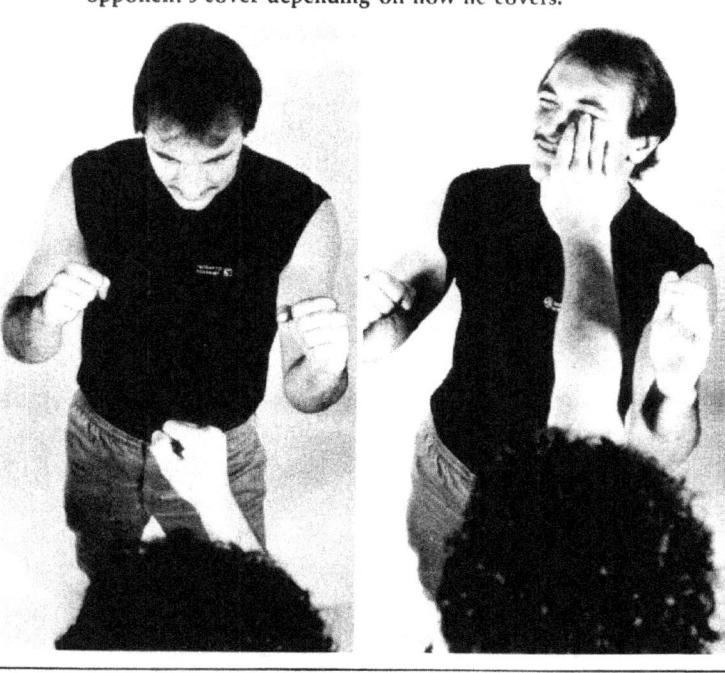

Hitting on the outside line

7. The angle of the fist on impact can vary. Experiment on this.

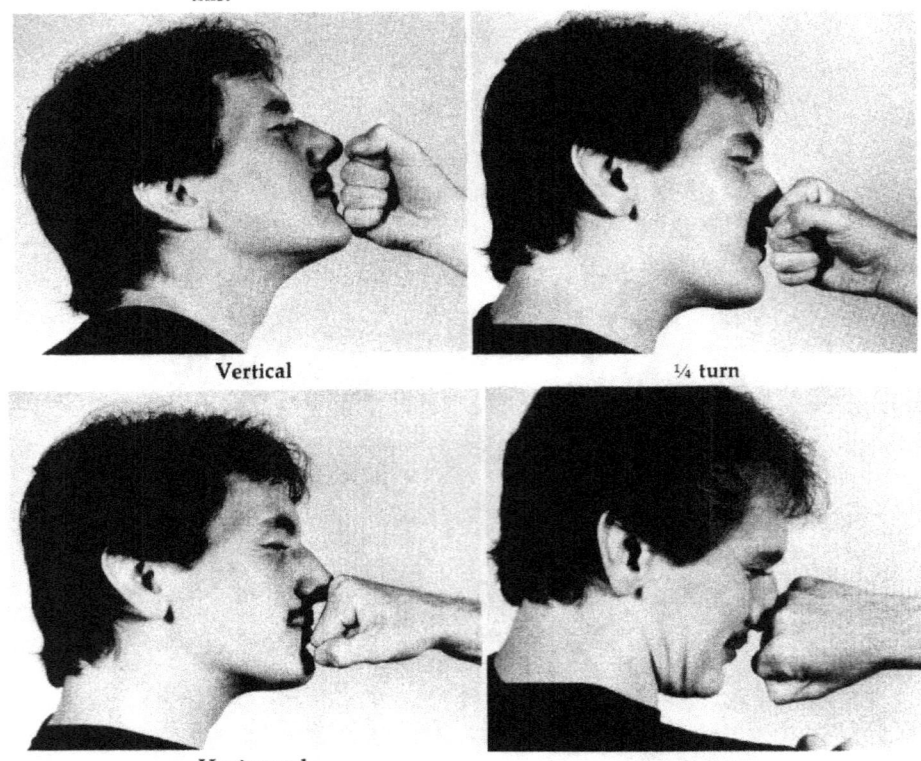

Vertical   ¼ turn

Horizontal   ¾ turn

8. Besides your fist you can hit with other areas of your hand.

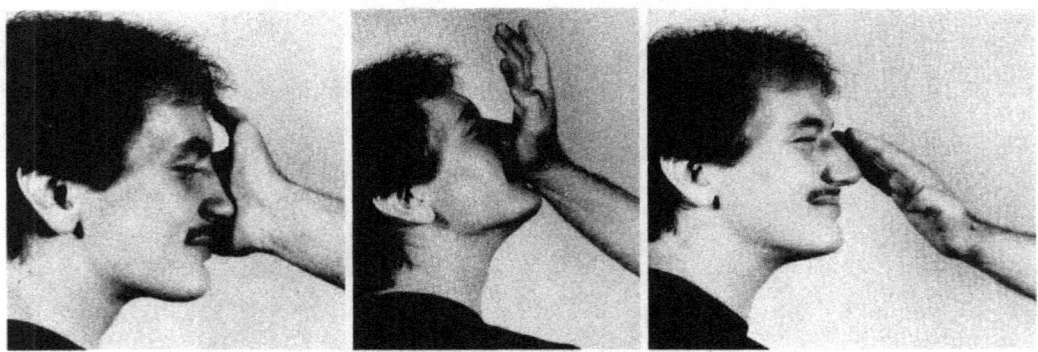

Jab with side palm   Jab with straight palm   Finger jab

MAJOR JAB ERRORS

Avoid the following errors when you jab:

First let's review the correct form for the jab

Correct jab side view

Correct jab front view

JAB ERRORS

1. Lifting the rear foot off of the ground will weaken your punch and make it more difficult to recover.

2. Lowering your rear guard will not add to your power and will leave you open to a counterattack.

3. Dropping your front shoulder will also leave you open. If you drop your front shoulder and your rear guard, your whole head will be exposed.

4. If you cross your centerline you will be open to a rear hand counter.

5. If you drop your front hand after you jab, you will also create an opening.
6. If you raise your elbow you will weaken the punch and expose your ribs to a counterattack.

JAB TO THE BODY

While the body jab is usually used as a probe or a fake, it can be effective as the first punch in a combination attack.

The body jab side view

To do a body jab from a right lead. While stepping forward with your right foot drive your fist into your opponent's ribs. Make sure you angle to your left and cover the right side of your head with your rear hand. By angling and covering you make it more difficult for your opponent to counterattack.

Rear view

THE LEAD HOOK

The lead hook to the head can be thrown at three ranges.

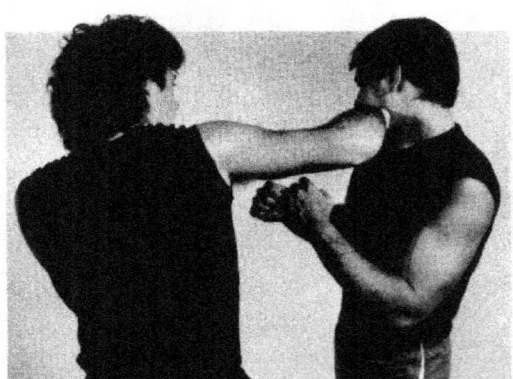

Tight hook

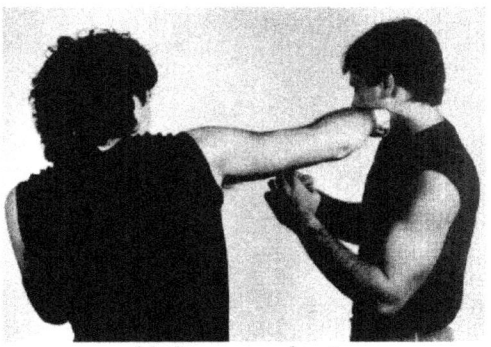

Medium range hook

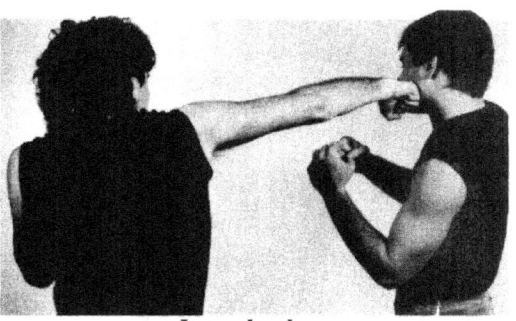

Loose hook

Which hook you use depends on your distance to your target. Whichever hook you throw, the principles of how you throw it will remain the same. To throw the hook drop your rear heel to the ground as you lift your front heel off the ground. At the same time pivot your hip to the right as you raise your right elbow and punch. As you throw a hook punch imagine you are turning in a barrel. When you hook make sure your arm is parallel to the ground and that your rear hand covers the left side of your head.

Your power will come from the weight transfer to your rear leg and the pivot of your hip.

The angle of your fist on impact can be:

Vertical

Or horizontal

COMMON HOOK ERRORS

The correct hook (tight front view)

ERRORS:

Turning the front foot over will weaken the punch because you are no longer punching "from the ground."

Too much follow through will leave you too open for a counterattack.

Too wide a swing will also leave you open.

Having your shoulder too far forward will also weaken the punch.

The correct angle of the shoulder

If the elbow is down the hook will be weaker and easier to block.

Correct angle of elbow.

THE SHOVEL HOOK

The shovel hook is a close range punch. As you punch you drop your weight on your foot as you lift your front heel off of the ground. The front hand shoots at an angle to the ribs or solar plexus. The action is similar to unloading a heavy shovel full of dirt. The shovel hook is almost always a body punch.

THE UPPERCUT

The target for the uppercut can either be the body or the chin. Like a shovel hook, the uppercut is also a close range weapon used for infighting. It is thrown just like the shovel hook, except it comes straight up while the shovel hook angles in.

THE BACK FIST

The classical back fist

The problem with the classical back fist is that when you cock the hand back you leave yourself open to your opponent's rear hand.

The JKD back fist

The JKD backfist is more efficient. Instead of cocking your hand back, bring your hip forward as you put your weight onto your front leg. This will give you the speed, the power, and the angle to make this an efficient tool for combat.

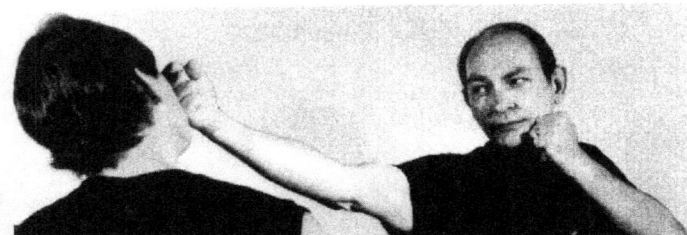
The back fist can be done with the knuckles.

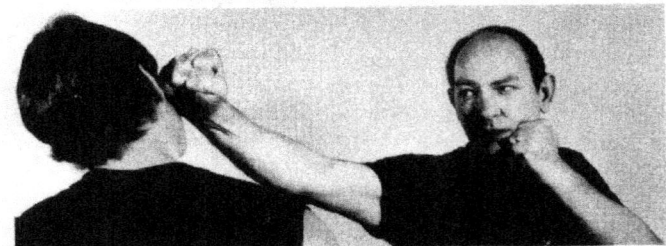
But since you can injure the back of your hand if you come in contact with your opponent's skull, it is recommended that you use a hammer fist.

THE STRAIGHT REAR (CROSS)

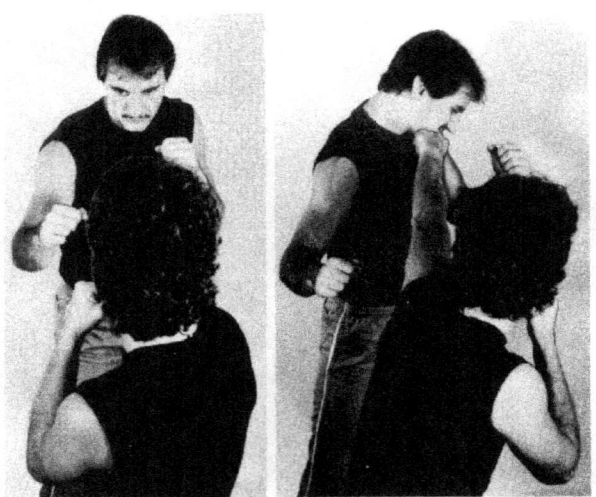
The straight arrow

The straight rear, also called the straight arrow, is a powerful punch. To throw this punch pivot your rear foot as you shoot your hand directly to your opponent's chin or nose. The whole left side of your body should act like a slamming door. The power comes from the pivot of the rear foot which pivots the rear hip which transfers the weight to the front leg. Unlike the classical reverse punch, the straight rear extends the shoulder. This shoulder extension adds power and distance to your punch.

THE CROSS

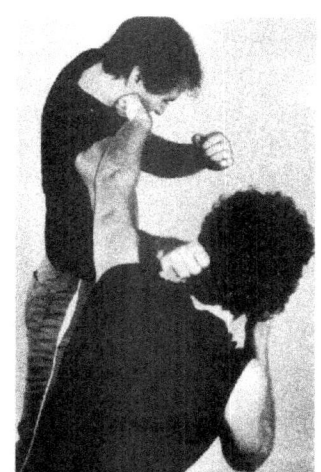

The cross is thrown when your opponent attempts to jab you. It requires a lot of practice and perfect timing to work. It is thrown just like a straight rear except it curves slightly as it "crosses" over your opponent's lead jab. You should slip inside your opponent's jab as your opponent crosses.

THE OVERHEAD

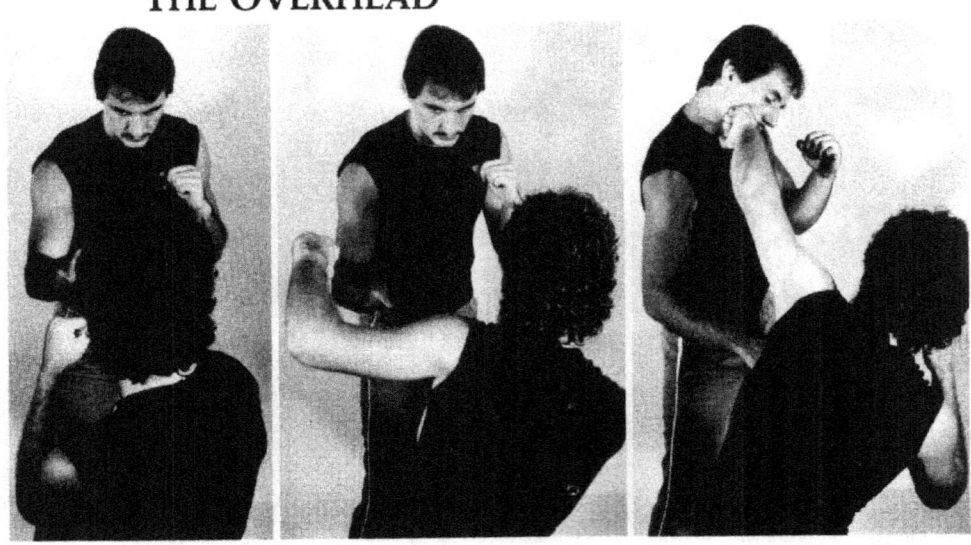

The overhead is thrown just like the straight arrow except the elbow raises and the punch loops to the target. The power comes from the momentum of your body as it drives forward.

THE LOW CROSS

To the inside line

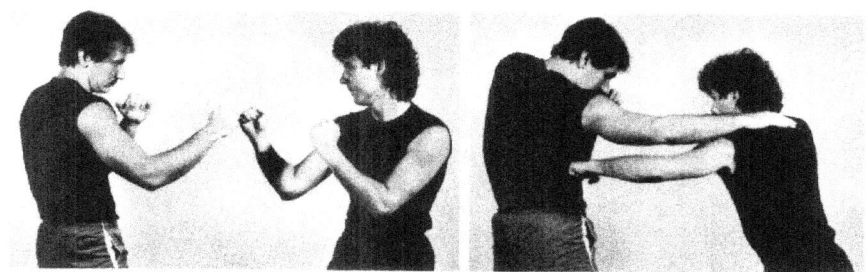

To the outside line

THE REAR HOOK TO THE HEAD

This is thrown just like the lead hook, except that it is almost always a tight hook and you twist your rear foot to get power.

REAR SHOVEL HOOK

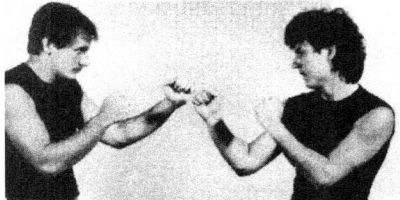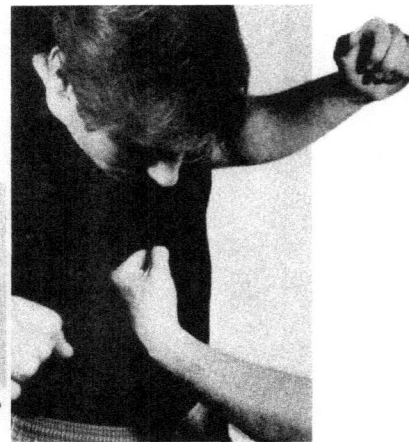

This is the same as the lead shovel hook except that the rear heel lifts up as the weight transfers to the front leg.

REAR UPPERCUT

The body mechanics of the rear uppercut are the same as the rear shovel hook.

REAR BACK FIST

To get the proper angle to throw the rear back fist twist your body to the right and transfer your weight to your front foot as you throw your rear hip into the punch.

BASIC USE OF FOCUS GLOVES

The focus glove is one of the most valuable pieces of training equipment available today. If used correctly, you can come very close to actually sparring, and use every possible punch. "Feeding" the focus gloves is an art in itself. A good feeder can use the gloves to make his partner work both offensive and defensive punching actions, develop his sense of timing, learn correct distancing for his punches, and increase mobility.

In the following examples we start from a stationary position with the gloves set, in order for the partner to learn visual recognition (what punches can be thrown at each glove when it is in a particular position). Then we progress to showing the glove to the partner from a neutral position (similar to using "flash cards" in school).

Training with the focus gloves can be done with: (a) the feeder remaining stationary, and (b) the feeder moving around. You are only limited by your own imagination in how to use the gloves.

STATIONARY FOCUS GLOVE

Holding the focus glove to practice distance and power of the various hand tools.

1. Jab or Cross

Front view   Side view

2. Jab, Cross, Hook
   or Jab, Hook, Cross
   or Jab, Hook
   or Cross, Hook

Front view   Side view

3. Jab, Cross, Low Hook
   or Jab, Low Hook, Cross

4. Jab, Cross, Uppercut

5. High Jab, Low Cross or High to Low Jab

Front view

Side view

6. Front and Rear Uppercuts

7. Low to High Hook

HITTING THE FOCUS GLOVE WITH A SINGLE DIRECT ATTACK (SDA)

1. The Jab

2. The Cross

3. The Hook

4. The Uppercut

THE FOCUS GLOVE FOR REACTION TRAINING

The focus glove can be used for stimulus-response training. This type of training is for speed, reaction, and speed of choice of the proper tool. To do this type of training hold the focus gloves in a neutral position with the rear glove on your chest and the front glove on your front thigh. Then move the glove or gloves to one of the examples shown.

HOW TO FEED FOR SINGLE DIRECT ATTACK (SDA)

1. Jab or Cross

2. High Hook

3. Low Hook

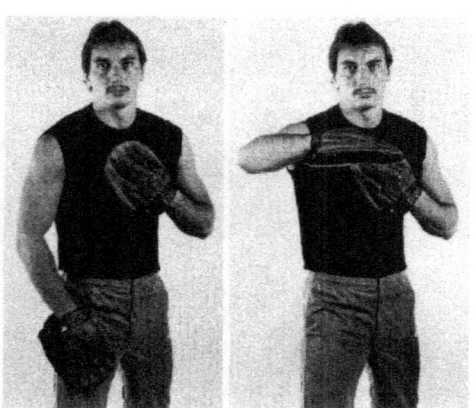

4. Uppercut

OUTSIDE PARRY AND HIT HEAD (OUTSIDE)

Sometimes an opponent will drop his lead after punching. This time as the opponent throws his lead jab, defender uses a rear cross parry, but returns his own high lead to the outside of opponent's lead arm.

INSIDE PARRY AND HIT HEAD

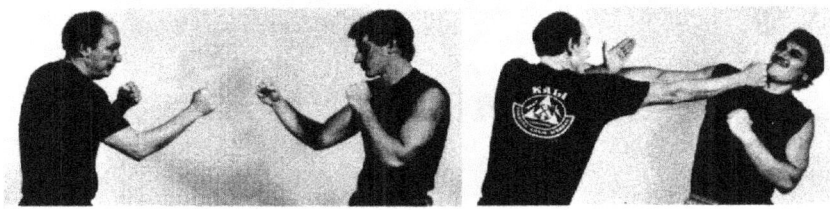

The lead jab is deflected with the rear hand as the defender shifts to the inside position and counters with his own lead jab. (Be careful anytime you move to the inside position as you are vulnerable to opponent's rear hand.)

CROSS PARRY AND FINGER JAB

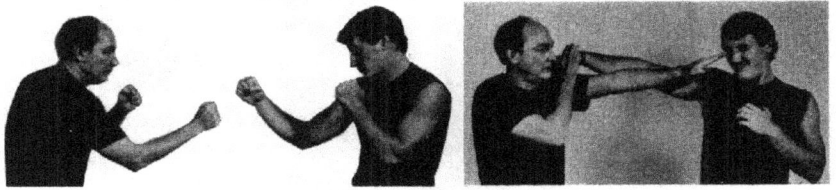

As the lead jab is thrown, defender twists his upper body as he uses a lead hand cross parry and counters with a rear hand finger jab to opponent's eyes.

DOUBLE LOW PARRY

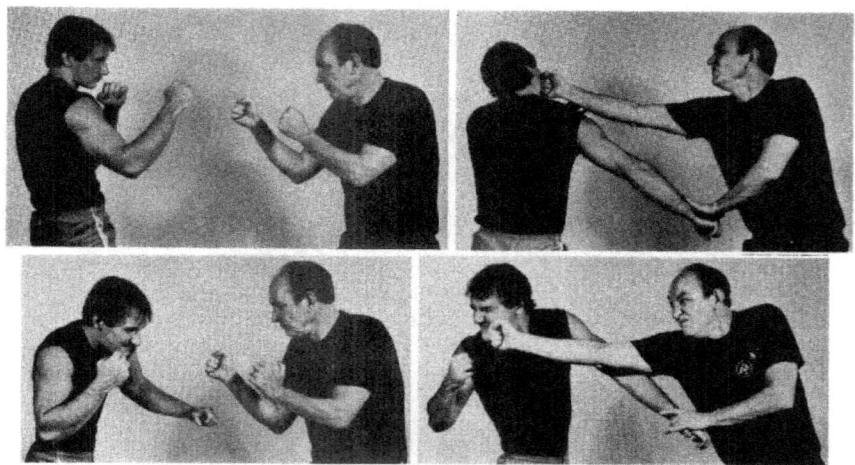

Opponent attempts to throw a low lead jab—rear cross. Defender parrys the jab with his rear hand and counter jabs with his lead hand. As rear cross is thrown he uses the same rear hand parry while countering with another lead punch.

PASS AND UPPERCUT

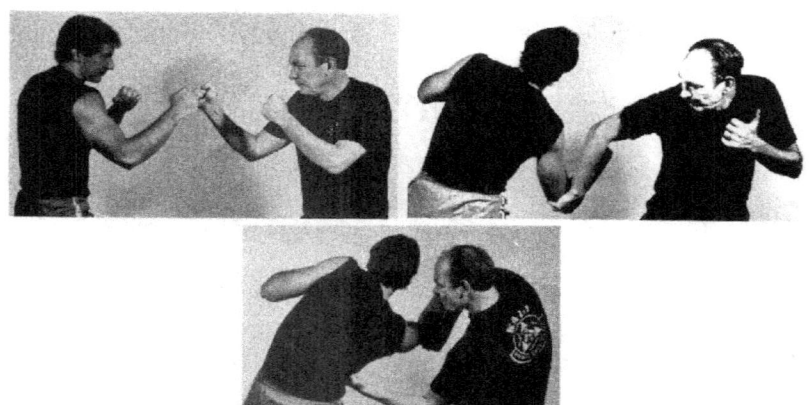

As opponent throws a shovel hook, defender drops lead hand, cupping opponent's arm and sweeping it outwards, then counters with his own shovel hook. (Sometimes combined with a sidestep to increase safety factor.)

EVASION
SLIP OUTSIDE

Opponent throws a lead jab. Just before impact the defender slips to the outside position, displacing his body from the punch, and is ready to counter.

SLIP INSIDE

Defender slips to the inside position, ready to counter. (Note high guard position in case opponent throws rear hand.)

SLIP OUTSIDE WITH COVER

the defender uses a rear hand cover as an added safety factor.

SLIP INSIDE WITH COVER

the defender uses a lead hand cover as an added safety factor.

DUCKING

FRONT HOOK

Defender ducks under opponent's lead hook by bending legs and shifting trunk slightly forward, hands held high and eyes watching opponent, ready to counter with either hand or defend.

REAR HOOK

Defender ducks under rear hook using the same motion as previously described, allows the blow to continue on its way, ready to counter or defend as necessary.

(In ducking one should be aware of not only possible hand follow-ups by the opponent, but also use of the rear leg, knee or elbow.)

(USING DISTANCE)
SNAP AWAY AGAINST JAB

As opponent flicks out a lead jab, defender shifts weight to his rear leg as he snaps his upper body out of distance and prepares to cover with his rear hand if necessary.

Note: This must be an extremely fast motion, otherwise there is a danger of being caught by a rear cross.

SHOULDER ROLL AGAINST REAR CROSS

As opponent's rear cross comes out, the defender shifts his weight to his rear leg and rolls backwards away from the punch. The chin is kept well tucked, behind the lead shoulder, eyes watching the opponent, arms covering the body and face.

BOBBING AND WEAVING

The following sequence of photographs illustrate the basic body mechanics of the bob and weave against an opponent, in matched leads.

From the ready position, and making it one smooth motion, bob forward by bending at the knees and waist, hands high and well covered, ready to slip at any time if necessary. Then weave to the outside position, ready to counter. Sometimes a sidestep is added with the weave to achieve a more favorable position to counter.

The mechanics are the same as above only this time you weave to the inside position.

BOB AND WEAVE TO OUTSIDE AGAINST LEAD HOOK

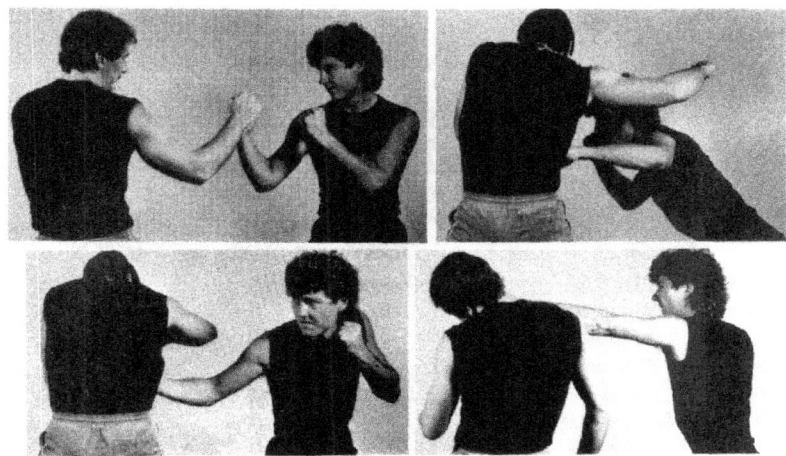

As opponent launches a lead hook bob forward to the inside position, hitting midsection with a tight rear cross (or hook), weave to the outside position and score with a body hook, followed immediately by a high rear cross.

BOB AND WEAVE AGAINST REAR CROSS

Opponent throws a high rear cross, defender bobs to the inside position and scores with a lead straight punch to the opponent's midsection, then weaves to the outside position and scores with a rear uppercut.

INTERCEPTION

An intercepting hit and parry can be done three ways.

COVER AND THEN HIT

Opponent throws a lead jab. Defender covers the line and returns his own lead punch.

SIMULTANEOUS COVER AND HIT

This time defender covers the lead jab of the opponent and returns his own lead punch simultaneously.

HIT FOLLOWED BY COVER

This time the defender anticipates the opponent's lead jab and beats him to the punch, then covers the opponent's jab as a follow-up if necessary.

STOP KICK AGAINST LEAD JAB

As opponent throws a lead jab, defender intercepts his attack with a stop-kick to the knee while shifting his own body out of range of the jab.

STOP HIT AGAINST KICK

As opponent launches a rear hook kick, defender intercepts his attack with a lead straight punch to the face.

STOP HIT AGAINST KICK WITH LOW COVER

Same as above only this time the defender closes the distance and covers the low line as he hits.

STOP KICK AGAINST KICK

As opponent launches a rear straight kick, defender counters by intercepting his attack with a stop kick to the opponent's leg.

Below are some examples of reaction training in action.

1. Cross

2. Cross to High Hook

From here on the neutral position will not be shown.

3. Jab to Low Hook

4. Cross to Uppercut

5. Jab, Uppercut, Uppercut, Hook

BASIC FOOT TOOL DEVELOPMENT

The use of the leg as a striking tool offers two major advantages. The first is longer reach, which enables you to score an attack from a greater distance. The second is more power, for it is a basic physiological fact that the legs are naturally much stronger than the arms. This is why we sometimes refer to the legs as heavy artillery.

Unfortunately, when it comes to kickboxing, most fighters resort to always slugging with their feet, as opposed to boxing with them.

As with punching, different kicks can be used to accomplish different goals. Some kicks may be used as minor attacks in order to set up a major attack, be it another kick or even a punch.

A good kicking repertoire makes it more difficult for an opponent to reach you with his hands, giving you a larger "aura of safety."

As with punching, kicking should be learned from a variety of angles, with both feet, and combined with footwork and body angulation.

THE STRAIGHT KICK

Below you can see the number of frames needed to do a straight kick in a classical manner. Bruce Lee felt that chambering the kick did nothing for power and made the kick inefficient by telegraphing it.

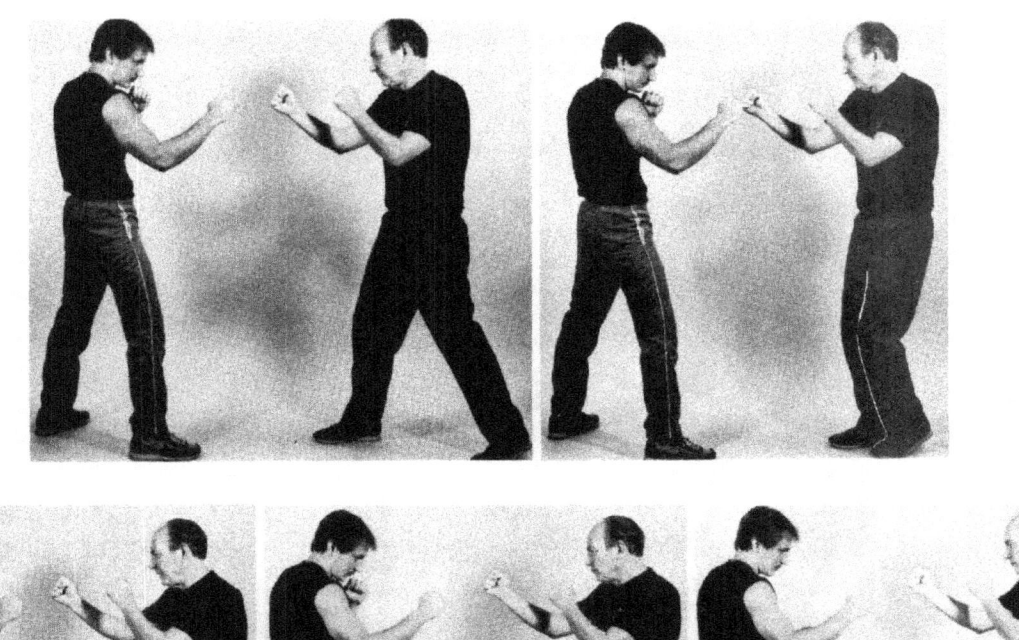

THE JKD STRAIGHT GROIN KICK

Slide up with your rear leg. At the same time snap your front leg up into your opponent's groin. Don't chamber the kicking leg. The bend of the knee will feel natural, don't worry about it. The power comes from a rising action of your hip as well as the short snap of your knee. Make sure you cover your head with your rear hand.

Kick with instep or shin

Kick with the toe

After your kick you can either bring your front foot back which will return you to your original position, or you can step directly down with your front foot as you use a hand attack.

THE FRONT THRUST KICK

This is the same as the snap kick except that the hip thrusts forward.

HOOK KICK

While most martial arts call this a roundhouse kick, we call it a hook kick because it follows the same line as a hook punch.

The classical roundhouse kick

There are less moves to the JKD hook kick. The power of the hook kick comes from the twisting action of your rear foot, the twist of your front hip, and the short snap of your knee. On any JKD kick hit through the target. Stay relaxed. DO NOT FOCUS. Keep your rear hand up to protect your head. Make contact with your toe, instep, or shin.

THE JKD HOOK KICK

To the groin with an upward angle

To the ribs with an inward or upward angle

To the neck with a downward angle

SIDE KICK

The basic side kick is done with the natural bend of the front knee as you slide your rear leg forward. The power comes from the hip as well as the body momentum moving forward. Again, don't focus. Hit through the target. Make contact with the flat of the heel or the whole flat of the foot.

If you work this kick it will become too powerful to use the classical blade of the foot to make contact as you can break your ankle.

THE JKD SIDE KICK

Down angle to shin or knee

Straight angle to body

Upward angle to face

The angle-in side kick

This is good to do when you are in an unmatched stance to your opponent. Step out with your right foot so that you can angle in to the exposed portion of your opponent's body, in this case his stomach.

THE INVERTED HOOK KICK

This kick is used as a front leg attack to the groin when you're in an unmatched stance. Slide up with your rear foot. Bring your front leg into your opponent's groin at an oblique angle. The power comes from the hip turning outward.

HEEL HOOK KICK

This kick can be done two ways, with whipping action of the knee or with a straight leg.

Straight leg heel hook kick

Whipping heel hook kick

Rear view

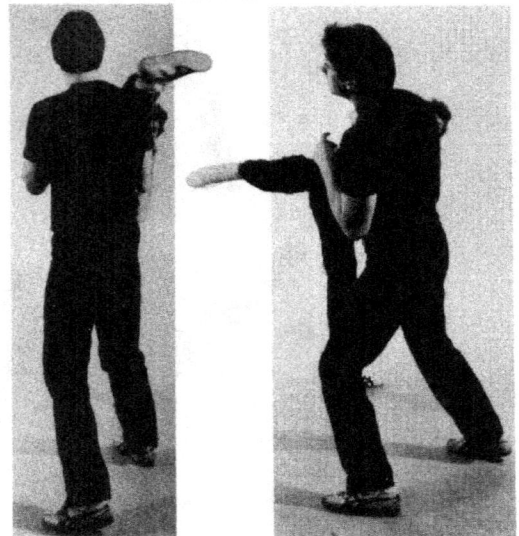

68

THE REAR LEG HOOK KICK

This is a power kick and is thrown similar to how the Thai boxers throw their round kick. The kick is usually thrown to the thigh, ribs or neck and the contact point is with your shin. The power comes from the twist of your front foot and the torque of your hip. As in any fully committed technique it is hard to fake or change the line with this kick. A good Thai boxer can generate a force of over 200 pounds with this kick.

The fully committed rear leg hook kick

The one half committed rear leg hook kick

This looks like the above kick except that the front foot does not torque as much, and the power is less. This kick is used as a probe, to bridge the gap, to fake or harass.

Quick rear hook kick with cover

This is a fast kick which returns to its original position. Make sure to retract the leg quickly.

REAR SIDE KICK

Since this is a relatively slow kick, it is seldom done above the knee.

STRAIGHT REAR

With step down into hand range

The power comes from your hip as well as the snapping action of your knee. Make sure you hit with your hand a split second before your foot hits the ground.

Retracting kick to stay out of hand range

If your opponent blocks your kick you can be in his hand range.

If you don't want to be in hand range, bring your kicking foot in front of your other foot.

OBLIQUE

The straight oblique comes from the floor to your opponent's knee with a lifting action.

With the stomping oblique you raise your rear knee and stomp down on your opponent's foot.

SPIN KICK

The spinning side kick

Spin on your front foot and do a side kick.

Side rear

If you extend your hip you do a side rear kick.

Spinning heel hook kick

This is a heel hook kick done from a spin.

FOOTWORK FOR FRONT LEAD KICK

The footwork you use for a kick depends on range, follow-ups or terrain.

Slide

Slide your rear foot forward as you kick.

Step and slide

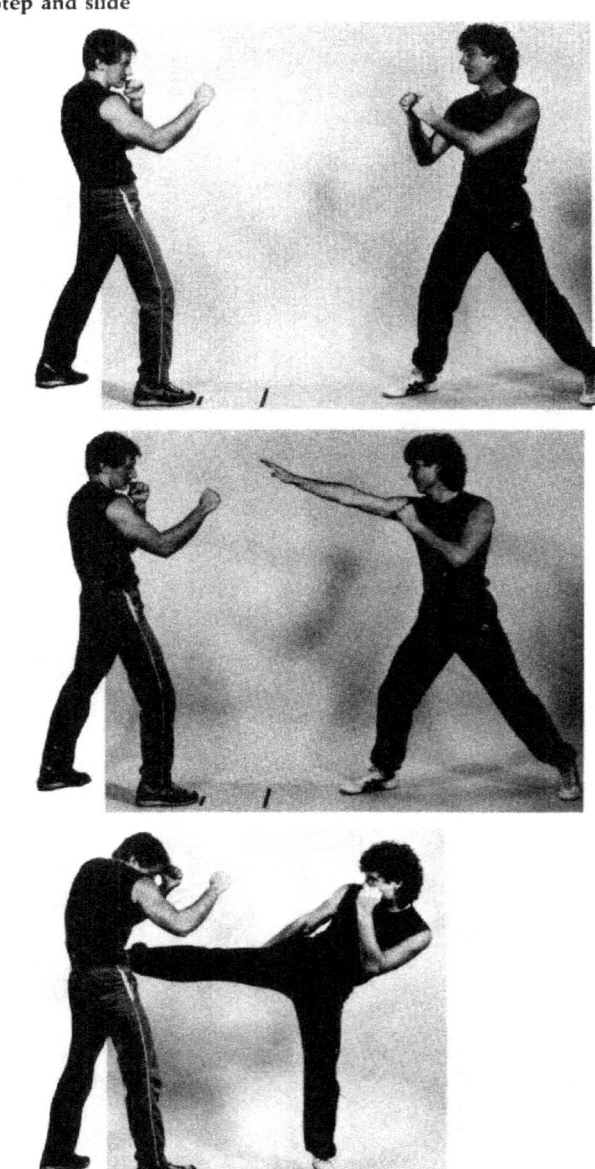

If you are too far away for a slide kick, take a short step forward with your front foot making sure you disguise the step with a front finger jab. Then slide and kick.

Pendulum

This is used to bridge the gap and return to your original position, thus staying out of hand range. After you slide and kick, bring your front foot back to your original position. In effect your front foot acts like the pendulum of a clock.

Lead switch

Slide up with the rear leg as you kick with the front. After you kick you can switch leads by bringing your front foot all the way back.

Cross in front and kick

While this footwork and the cross behind (see below) are structurally slower than the slide footwork, they should be learned because of terrain. Examples of terrain where the slide would be impractical would be an icy sidewalk, gravel, or any slippery or uneven surface.

To do the cross in front, simply cross in front with your rear leg and kick.

Cross behind

This is the same as the cross in front except that the rear leg crosses behind the front.

Usually a hook kick will "feel" better with a cross in front, and a side kick will "feel" better with a cross behind. This is because of the angle of your hip.

FOOTWORK FOR REAR LEG KICK

Step through

The step through bridges the gap and places you in hand range. Here we see a step through hook kick followed by a jab.

Retracting

The retracting allows you to kick with your rear leg and by bringing it back to your original position, you can stay out of hand range.

Lead switch with pendulum

By adding a pendulum with your kicking leg, you can stay out of hand range and switch leads.

BASIC USE OF TRAINING EQUIPMENT

The use of various types of training equipment for kicking is to aid in developing an immediate relationship to an opponent, a feel of hitting something. Each piece of equipment has advantages and disadvantages. But if used correctly, the equipment is invaluable for training one's kicking skills. The following sequences illustrate the training of basic kicks utilizing focus gloves and the kicking shield. Other equipment such as heavy bags, and Thai pads can and should be used also. In the beginning stages the equipment holder should remain in a stationary position, but once the martial artist is competent in using basic kicks, the holder should begin to move around as he sets different targets. This way the kicker learns to relate to a moving target.

Work on economical motions in delivering your kicks, quick recovery and well-covered positioning.

FOCUS GLOVE
SINGLE DIRECT ATTACK (SDA)
Front kick

Hook kick

Side kick

Inverted hook kick

Heel hook

KICKING SHIELD
SINGLE DIRECT ATTACK (SDA)
Front kick

Side kick

Hook kick

Inverted hook

Rear hook kick

Spin kick

ATTACK BY COMBINATION (ABC)

An attack by combination may be defined as a series of two or more attacking motions that flow from one to another naturally, and are usually thrown to more than one target area.

Utilizing the hands and feet either separately or in combination, they are compound attacks, employed in a well-planned series, with each opening creating another.

Although used in conjunction with feints and all other forms of attack such as single direct attack, in attack by combination each blow in the series is intended to score. This requires economical motion, tight defense, speed and surprise, and determination in execution.

Most combinations have a rhythmic feel to the series. However, the rhythm of any series can be varied by either speeding up or slowing down the tempo of one or more of the blows being thrown.

HAND-HAND (H-H)

Below are just a few of the many H-H combinations.

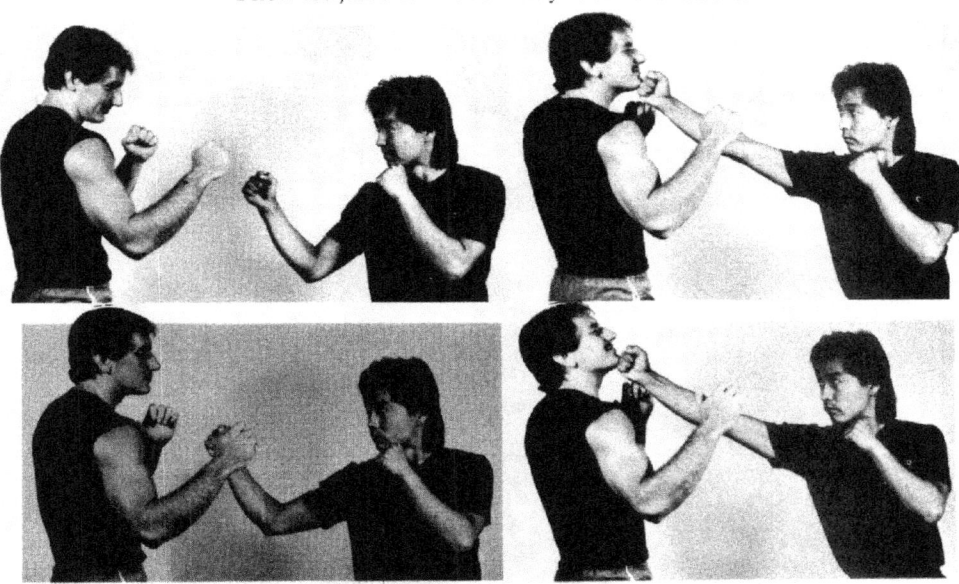

Double Jab

Low to High Jab

Jab to Cross

Jab to Low Cross

Jab to High Hook

HAND-FOOT (H-F)

Below are a few examples of (H-F) combinations.

Jab to Low Side Kick

Jab to Hook Kick

Jab to Inverted Hook Kick

Jab to Spin Kick

Jab to Rear Hook Kick

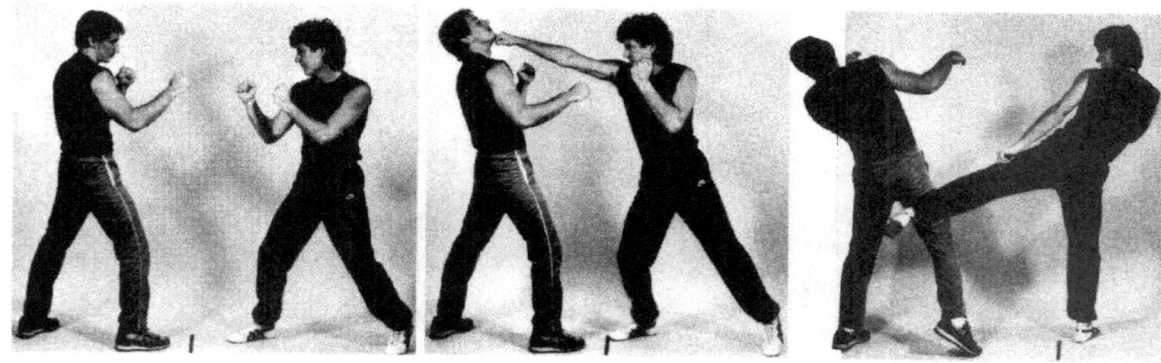

FOOT-HAND (F-H)

Below are just a few examples of possible (F-H) combinations.

Hook Kick to Jab

Hook Kick to Back Fist

Hook Kick to Hook Punch

ATTACK BY COMBINATION (ABC) FOOT-FOOT (F-F) USING FOCUS GLOVES

Below are just a few examples of how to use focus gloves for ABC kicking.

Front Kick to Hook Kick

After your front kick makes contact with the focus glove, your partner quickly places the glove in a vertical position, you then do a hook kick without your kicking foot touching the ground.

Another way to do this combination is to have your partner slide back after the front kick. You then have to plant your front foot and slide up and hook kick (not shown).

The first one would be a combination if your opponent stands and blocks. The second one is used if he retreats from your front kick.

Hook Kick to Side Kick

Front Hook Kick to Rear Hook Kick

F-F ON THE SHIELD

Front Hook Kick to Side Kick

Side Kick to Spin Kick

Front Hook Kick to Rear Hook Kick

HITTING THE FOCUS GLOVE WITH AN ATTACK BY COMBINATION (ABC)

Below are just three examples of the many ABC hand attacks that are possible.

Jab, Cross, Hook

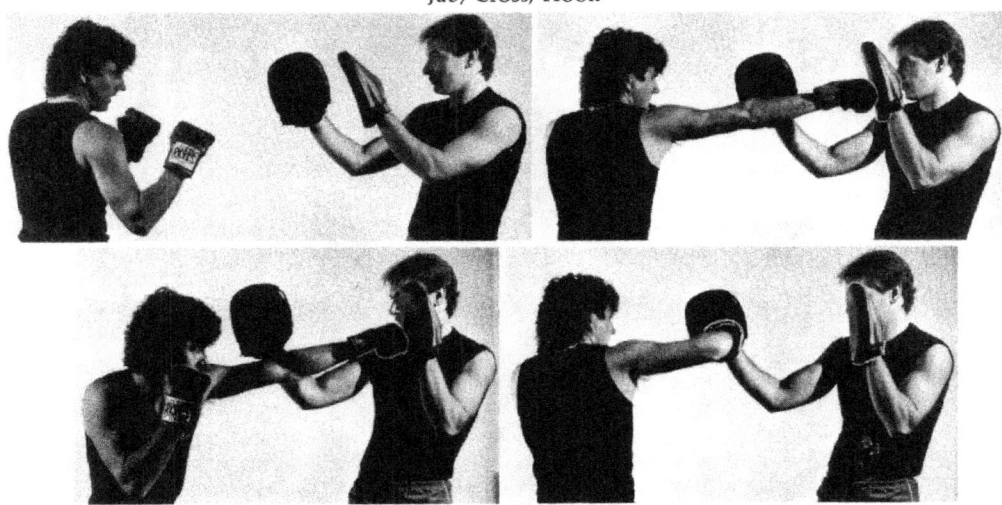

Jab, Hook, Cross

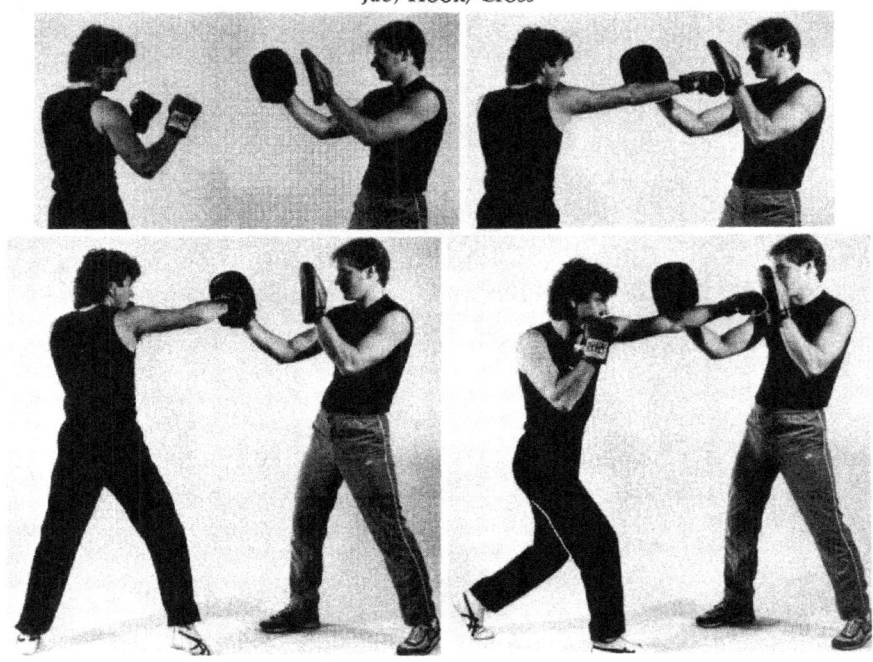

Jab, Cross, Uppercut

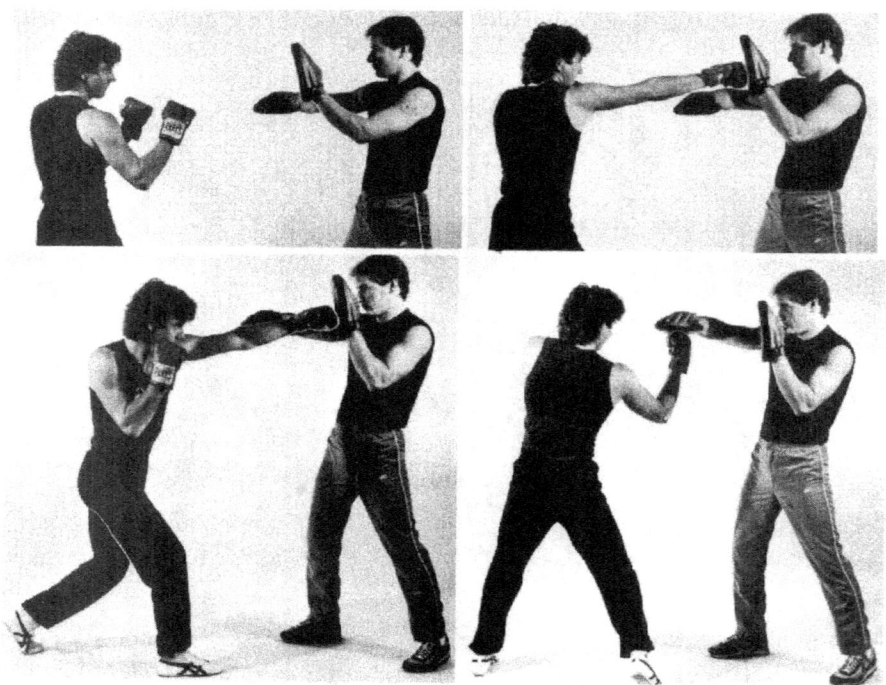

Some of the other stationary combinations you can practice are as follows:

1. Low Jab, High Lead Hook.
2. High Jab, Low Jab, High Hook.
3. High Jab, High Hook, Rear Uppercut.
4. High Jab, Rear Uppercut, High Hook.
5. High Jab, High Lead Hook, Rear Hook.
6. High Jab, Low Lead Hook, High Lead Hook.
7. Low Jab, Rear Hook.
8. Lead Uppercut, Rear High Hook.
9. Lead Hook, Lead Uppercut, Rear Hook.
10. Lead Uppercut, Rear Hook, Lead Hook.
11. Double Jab, any other Hit or Hits.
12. Lead Hook, Rear Hook, Lead Uppercut, Rear Uppercut.
13. Lead Uppercut, Lead Hook, Rear Uppercut, Rear Hook.
14. Cross to Body, High Lead Hook, Cross.
15. Cross to Body, Lead Hook to Body, Cross.

H-F AND F-H USING FOCUS GLOVES

Below are a few of the many combinations.

Jab to Hook Kick

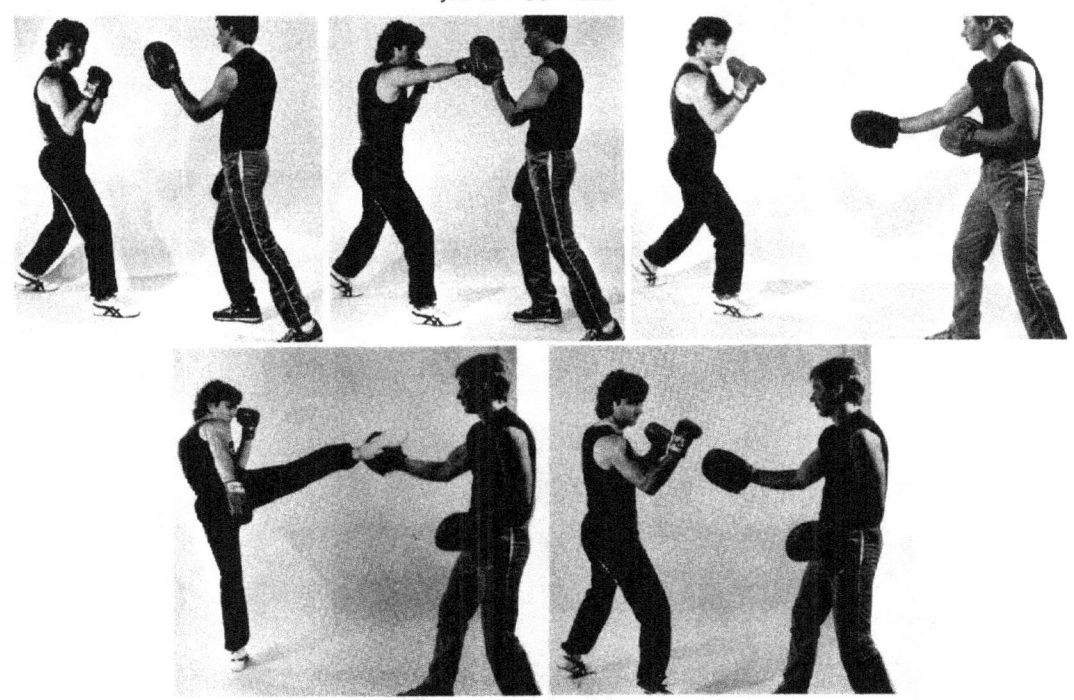

Hook Kick to Jab

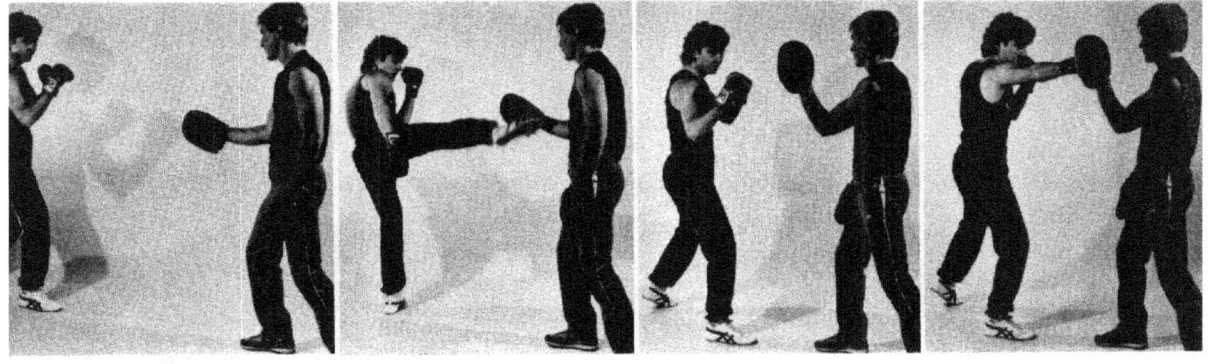

Back-Fist to Side Kick

H-H-F USING FOCUS GLOVES

Jab to Cross to Rear Hook Kick

PROGRESSIVE INDIRECT ATTACK (PIA)

Progressive indirect attack is differentiated from attack by combination in that, in PIA, only the final blow is intended to score. This method of attack can be very effective against an opponent whose defense is strong and fast, and who cannot be reached with simple attacks.

PIA uses feints and false attacks to draw a reaction from the opponent, to induce the execution of a block or some other defensive motion, then deceive the defensive move to score in an opening line.

PROGRESSIVE COVER DISTANCE:

Which means that your initial feint or false attack should bridge the distance to be closed by at least half, leaving your final motion only the last half of the distance.

INDIRECT COVERS TIME

You keep ahead of the opponent's defensive move, avoiding contact with the opponent on the feint as you complete your attack. But your feint must be made deep enough, and held long enough, so that the opponent will react to it.

It should be remembered that a progressive indirect attack is a single forward motion without withdrawal. Feints can be simple or compound, but too many motions allow too much time for the opponent to recover or counterattack. Subtlety is an essential ingredient for success—your final motion being economical and fast.

The opponent should be studied first with single attacks and feints to gain some idea as to how he will react in certain situations. The idea is to draw the opponent's defense in the opposite direction from where you want your final attack to land.

A danger of using PIA too frequently is that an opponent may appear to react a certain way during your feints, but then switch and counterattack on your real attack.

Progressive Indirect Attack (PIA) compared to Indirect Attack (IA).

INDIRECT ATTACK (IA)

An indirect attack will usually occur in two motions, the fake and the hit. In the example below a low punch is started toward the target (the fake). Then the fist is withdrawn and a high punch (the hit) is thrown.

PROGRESSIVE INDIRECT ATTACK (PIA)

With a PIA attack, the low punch does not withdraw, rather "progresses" toward the target. With a PIA the two motions are a part of the same motion.

The most common PIA attacks have the following variations:
1. From the low line to the high line
2. From the high line to the low line
3. From the inside line to the outside line
4. From the outside line to the inside line

Below are a few examples of some PIA attacks.

HAND-HAND (H-H) PIA ATTACKS

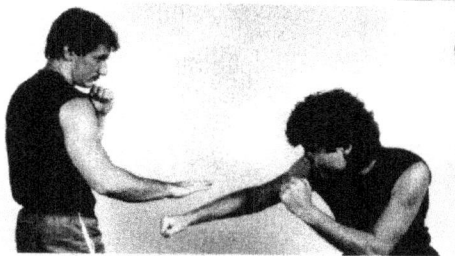 

Low Jab to High Jab

Low Jab to High Hook

Low Jab to Back Fist

HAND-FOOT (H-F) PIA ATTACKS
Finger Jab to Hook Kick

The hand does not withdraw before the kick.

Finger Jab to Shin Kick

The hand does not withdraw before the kick.

HAND-HAND-FOOT (H-H-F) PIA ATTACKS

Low Jab to High Jab to Rear Leg Hook Kick

Low Jab to High Jab to Side Kick

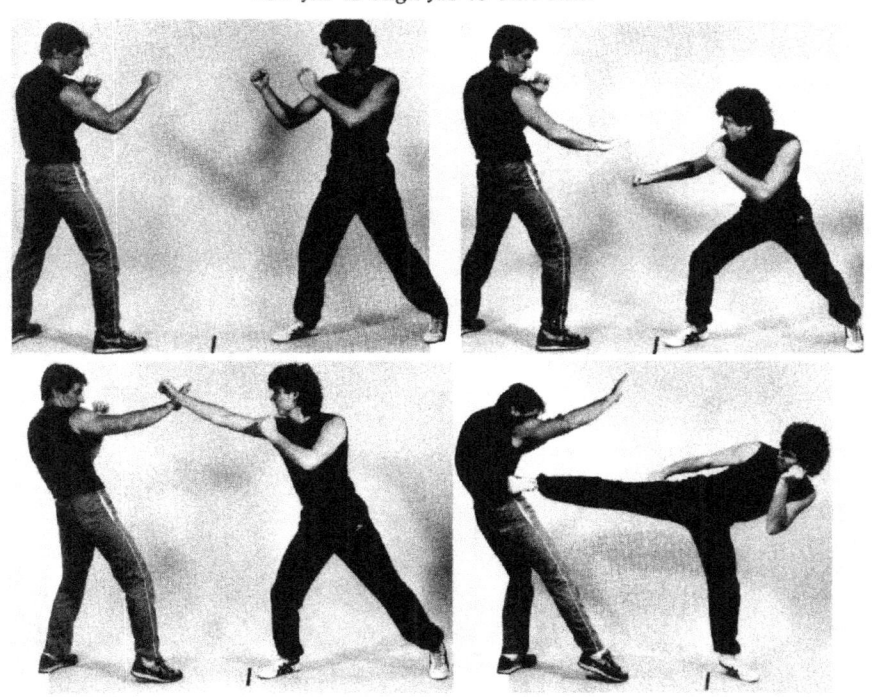

FOOTWORK TO PIA ATTACKS

Stationary to Stationary with Hit

Step to Stationary with Hit

Stationary to Step with Hit

Step to Step with Hit

Which footwork you use depends on distance between you and your opponent.

DEFENSIVE TOOLS AND DRILLS

There is a basic theory in fighting which states, "For every move there is a counter." Attack has been given priority in JKD, and is important, but so is defense. Defensive techniques can negate an opponent's attack and place you in a position to counter. The learning of defensive skills is necessary, and should include as wide a variety of defensive techniques as possible.

One of the main theories of defense in JKD is that the best form of defense is a good offense. Rather than attempting to block a kick or punch, the idea is to try to intercept it with your own kick or punch. This way even if the opponent's attack should score, at least there is an exchange. This requires a continual alertness and awareness of the opponent and his movements.

However, intercepting may not always be possible or appropriate. Perhaps one's awareness is off, you may not have time, then one's skill in defense may well make the difference between success and failure.

The basic methods of defense are listed, from the least to most efficient:

(1) **Distance**—Simply getting out of the way of the attack and allowing it to miss its target. This usually means that you will not be able to counterattack without first reclosing the distance.

(2) **Blocking and Hitting**—What is known as "touch and go." In this case the attack is halted with a definite blocking motion, and then the counterattack is launched.

(3) **Parrying and Hitting**—Differentiated from the previous method by the fact that rather than a pure block, a parry is used to dissolve or redirect the attack, then the counterattack is thrown.

(4) **Evasiveness**—Includes such body motions as slipping, ducking, bobbing and weaving in order to avoid an attack by misplacement, while remaining in range to counter.

(5) **Intercepting**—The opponent's attack is intercepted by the defender's own counterattack, nullifying the original attack.

As stated before, the method of defense chosen may depend upon the circumstances under which an attack is delivered. Sometimes distance may be more appropriate than interception, and vice versa. If you understand all the variables, you have a wider selection to choose from and will not be limited.

The following sequences offer examples of the defensive methods just described, with the exception of distance.

BLOCKING AND HITTING
SHOULDER STOP AGAINST WIDE REAR CROSS

   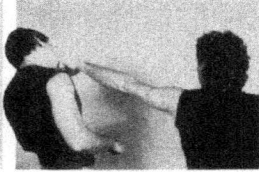

As the opponent starts to throw a wide rear cross, the defender snaps out his lead hand to shove the opponent's shoulder, disrupting the opponent's punch, then counters immediately with his own rear cross.

Closeup insert of shoulder stop (can be used on opponent's bicep if shoulder is too far away).

SHOULDER STOP AGAINST REAR OVERHEAD

As opponent launches a rear overhead, the defender uses the same shoulder stop. (Note defender's rear hand is kept well up and guarding against opponent's possible lead hand punch.)

CUT INTO REAR UPPERCUT

As opponent throws a rear uppercut to the solar plexus, the defender lowers his lead elbow and wedges his lead arm onto the uppercut, then immediately counters with a rear uppercut. (Note how defender keeps himself covered and is aware of opponent's other hand.)

FOREARM BLOCK FRONT UPPERCUT

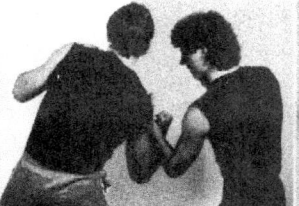

As opponent loops a lead uppercut to the solar plexus, the defender twists his body, dropping his rear forearm into the crook of the opponent's elbow, smothering the punch, immediately follows with a lead hook to the opponent's head.

COVER AGAINST LEAD HOOK TO HEAD

As opponent throws a high lead hook, defender shifts forward into the circumference of the blow, and covers with his rear hand, immediately follows with his own lead hook counter. (Be very aware of opponent's rear hand and elbow when you are in this position.)

PARRYING AND HITTING

OUTSIDE PARRY AND HIT BODY

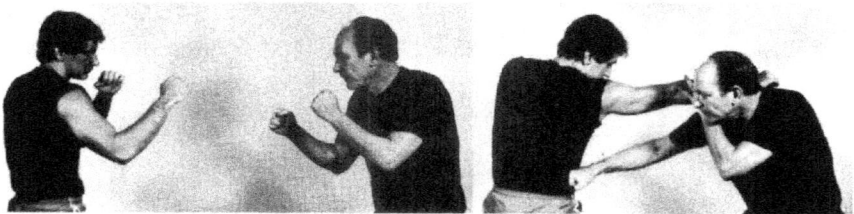

Opponent throws a lead jab. Just before it lands defender uses a cross parry with his rear hand, deflecting the punch over his lead shoulder while returning a low lead punch to opponent's stomach (defender shifts his body slightly left as an added safety measure).

OUTSIDE PARRY AND HIT HEAD (INSIDE)

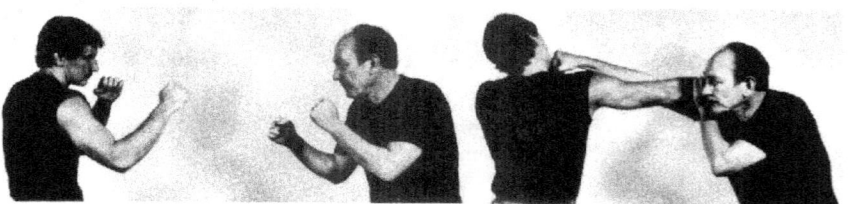

Same parry as above but this time the defender returns a high lead punch inside opponent's guard.

SLIDING LEVERAGE AGAINST JAB

As opponent jabs, defender bridges across the outside of opponent's arm, simultaneously deflecting the punch and countering with a finger jab to the eyes. (This is a sliding motion which maintains contact with opponent's arm throughout.)

SLIDING LEVERAGE AGAINST REAR CROSS

As opponent throws a rear cross, defender bridges across the opponent's arm with his own rear sliding leverage, simultaneously deflecting the blow and countering.

SLIDING LEVERAGE AGAINST UPPERCUT

As opponent launches a lead uppercut to the midsection, defender lowers his body slightly, cuts into the punch and counters with his own punch.

CATCH AND RETURN JAB

As opponent jabs, defender catches the punch with his rear guard hand, then returns his own jab as the opponent's arm retracts.

SIMULTANEOUS CATCH AND JAB

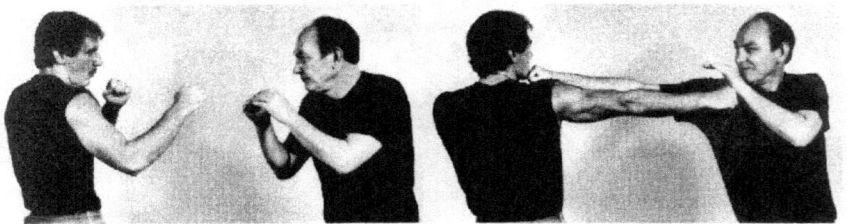

This time the catch and return jabs are used simultaneously.

CATCH AND CROSS PARRY AGAINST JAB AND CROSS

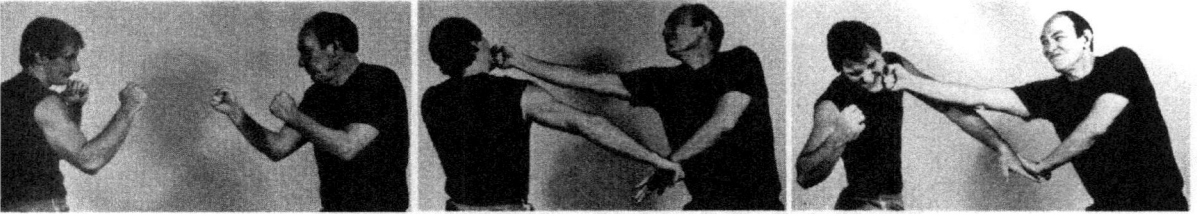

As opponent jabs to the low line, defender simultaneously catches and returns a high jab, then cross parrys the opponent's low cross while scoring with another high straight punch.

COUNTER ATTACKING

A counterattack is an attack made as the opponent is attacking, or is about to. It can be divided into three timings.

(1) Before the movement—While the opponent is preparing to launch an attack (attack on preparation) possibly by advancing with footwork.

(2) During the movement—While the attack is under development but has not reached its target (outgoing).

(3) After the movement—As the attack reaches complete extension, or even as it is retracting (chambering).

The following sequence of photographs illustrates the various timings as used against a lead jab-rear cross attack.

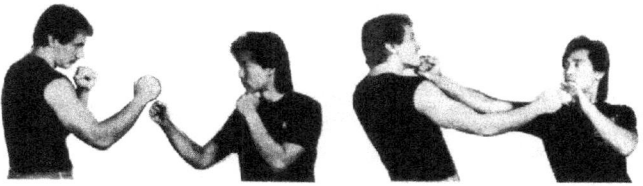

As opponent begins to throw the lead jab, defender counterattacks before and intercepts motion with his own lead punch, thus nullifying the attack at the start.

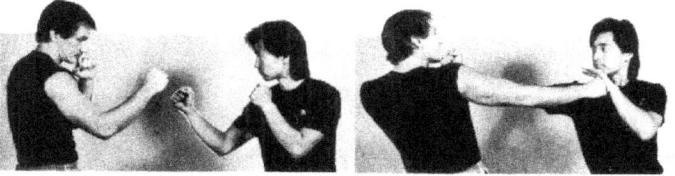

This time the defender simultaneously catches the jab and counters with his own jab.

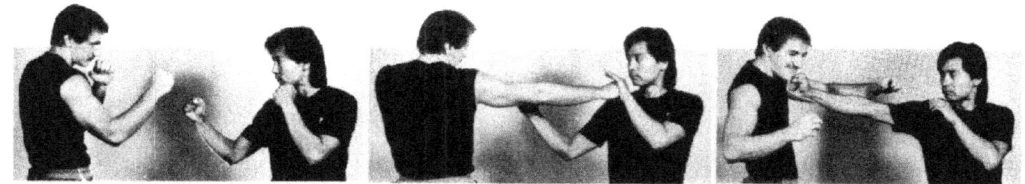

The defender catches the opponent's lead jab, then stop-hits as the cross is coming.

The lead jab is caught and the defender simultaneously parries the rear cross and hits.

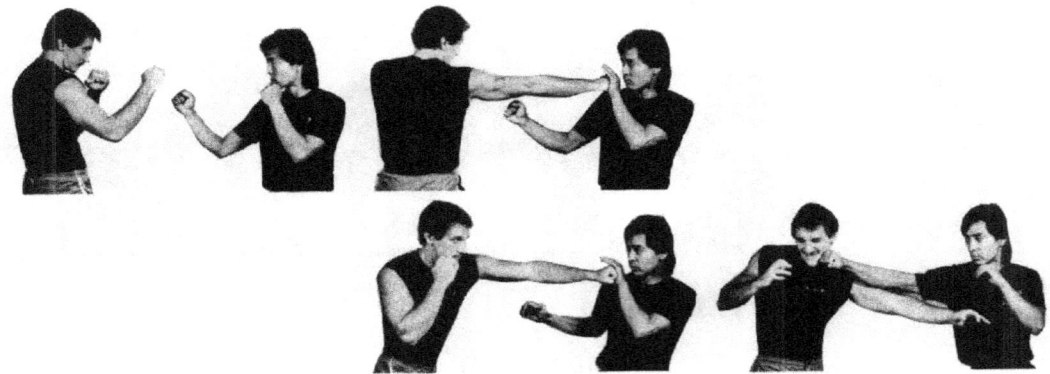

The defender catches the lead jab and rear cross, then counters to the opponent's face.

The defender catches the jab, parries the rear cross, then counter hits.

USING FOOT DEFENSIVE TOOLS

As opponent is beginning to initiate a kicking attack, the defender intercepts the attack with a stop-kick, followed by a finger jab as the distance is closed.

As the opponent's kick is on its way, the defender uses footwork and body angulation to avoid the kicking leg and cuts the opponent's support leg with a counter kick.

As opponent side kicks, defender closes range and parries the kick while simultaneously stop-kicking opponent's support leg.

If opponent pendulum side kicks, defender pendulum shifts back and parries the kick as it reaches full extension, then follows with a pendulum side kick to opponent's returning leg.

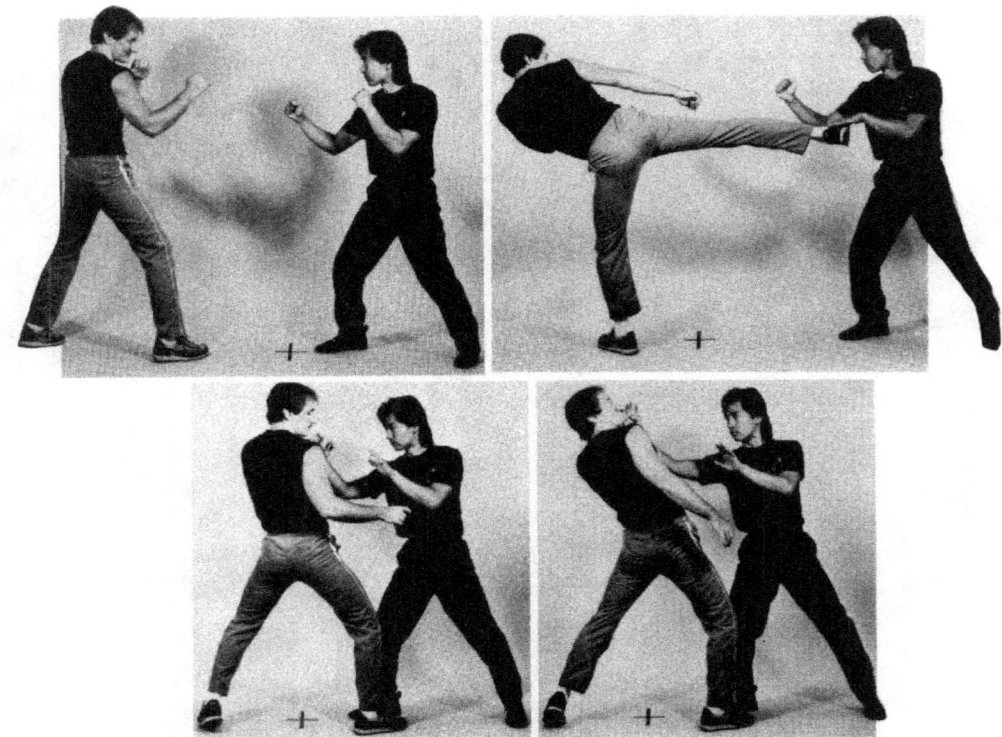

If opponent side kicks and plants his weight forward, defender uses a slide-step retreat and parries the kick at full extension, then crashes opponent's line with a lead punch.

Timing and distance are important if you want to be in range to counterattack successfully.

The same defensive concepts illustrated can be used against combination attacks using: hand-foot, foot-foot, or foot-hand attacks.

DEFENSIVE USE OF FOCUS GLOVE

The focus glove can also be used to:
1. **Block and counterattack.**
2. **To check your cover.**
3. **To work on slipping and the bob and weave.**

Some examples of the defensive use of focus gloves:

Inside parry the jab to jab

When your training partner jabs or does a loose hook with the front focus glove, bring up your rear hand to inside parry the attack then return a jab.

Shoulder roll the cross to return cross and uppercut.

When your partner hits you with a rear focus glove, put your weight on your rear leg and roll away from the punch. Quickly return a cross followed by an uppercut.

Jab to cover low cross.

After you jab your partner returns a low cross. Quickly bring your elbow down to cover the punch.

Jab to cover low jab.

After you jab, your partner returns a low jab. Cover it with your rear elbow.

Inside slip the jab to high hook

When your partner jabs, slip inside the jab and return a high hook. Notice how the man who jabs returns the glove to hook position.

Outside slip jab to cross

Slip outside of the jab and return a cross.

Bob and weave under front hook to low hook and cross return.

When your partner does a hook with the focus glove, bob to the inside. Then quickly weave under the arm, hook to the body as you come up from the weave. Follow this with a cross.

Bob and weave under rear hook to uppercut, hook

Bob inside his rear hook. Weave to the outside, then uppercut the body and hook to the focus glove.

Cover low hook to double uppercut.

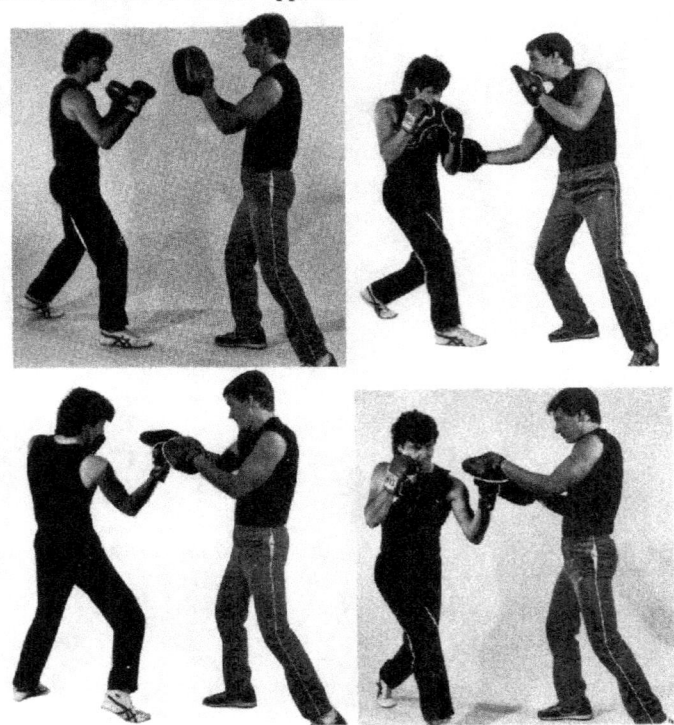

When your partner does a low hook, cover it with your rear elbow followed by two uppercuts.

You should practice all of the above until you can react instantly. Then you should mix the drills so that you block and hit or hit and then block. Be as inventive as possible. Work the focus gloves until you and your partner make it as close to sparring as possible.

ATTACK BY DRAWING (ABD)

Attack by drawing is essentially counterfighting. It is initiated by "baiting" an opponent into a commitment. By offering him an apparent opening, or by executing an action that he may attempt to time and counter, and then to counterattack as he "takes the bait."

You can draw an opponent's commitment by:

(a) Exposing a target to the opponent (invitation).
(b) Forcing a reaction (as in crashing a particular line).
(c) Feinting (to draw a reaction).

The first method (invitation) is DEFENSIVE—in that the intent is to cause the opponent to attack under certain conditions so as to know the exact sector the attack will arrive in. The other methods (forcing and feinting) are OFFENSIVE—in that the intention is to make the opponent react in a set manner and to develop an attack that takes into account either his defensive move or his counterattack.

In fencing, ABD is referred to as second-intention attack, and is very effective against a fighter who bases his game plan primarily on counterattack.

An important point to remember is that attack by drawing is a premeditated action and its success depends upon luring the opponent into attacking into the opening being offered. Subtlety is an essential ingredient then, for the action must achieve the desired result, that of drawing a specific reaction from the opponent. And though it must be a deliberate error, it must never appear so to the opponent or he will not take the opening. (Very experienced fighters will seldom, if ever, attack into an open sector if they have the slightest idea that it may be a setup.)

Correct timing and distance are extremely important in using ABD. If you are too close to the opponent, his attack may score before you have time to counter, and if you are too far away he may not react to the opening, or even if he does, distance will not allow your own counterattack to score.

Balance is necessary in your attack also, so as to be ready to counterattack or defend yourself if necessary.

The following examples illustrate various ways of using attack by drawing.

DIFFERENT HAND "BAITS."

The photos below show the "baits" in exaggerated form for clarity.

Defender lowers rear hand guard to expose head. Defender lowers lead hand guard to expose head. Defender raises rear elbow to expose body.

Defender raises both elbows to expose body. Defender holds both hands wide to expose interior body and head.

ATTACK BY DRAWING AGAINST HANDS

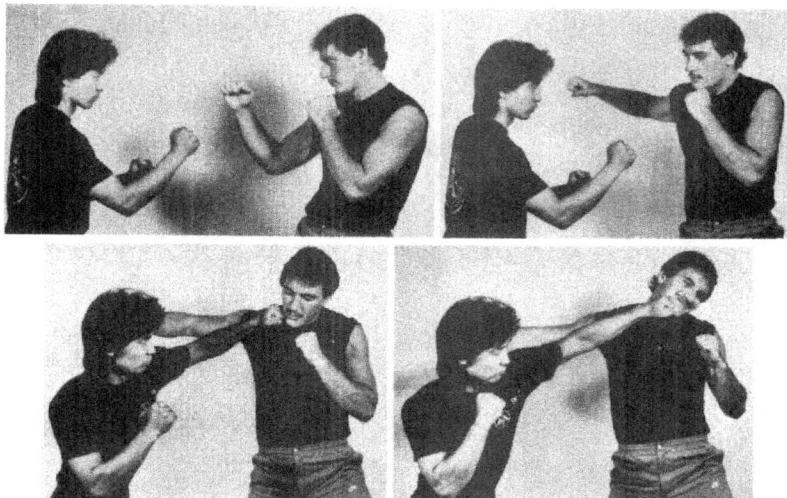

Defender lowers his rear hand guard slightly, drawing a lead hook from his opponent, which he counters by sidestepping and throwing a rear cross to opponent's face (lead hand held high to counter opponent's rear hand).

Defender lowers his lead hand to draw a lead punch from the opponent, which he counters by slipping outside and returning a high jab.

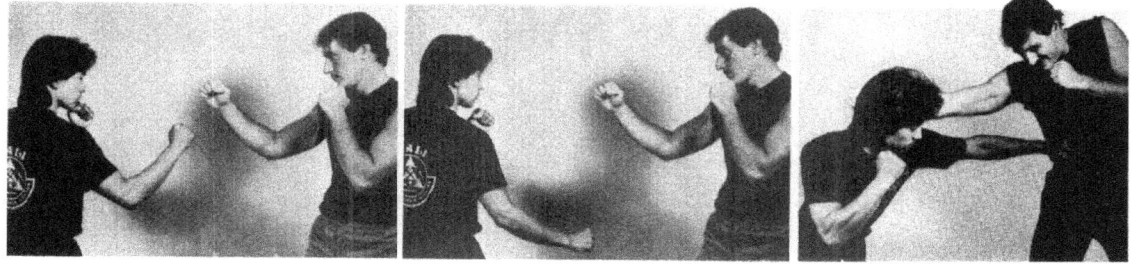

Dropping his lead hand, the defender baits the opponent's lead jab, then slips inside and counters with a rear cross to opponent's midsection.

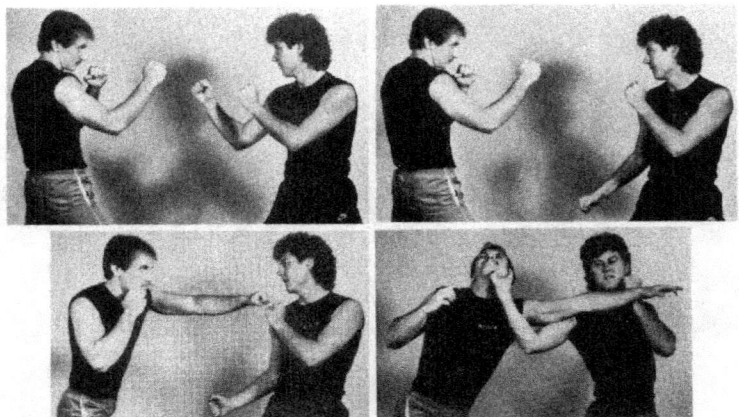

Lowering his lead hand, the defender baits a high rear cross, which he counters by angling his body and scoring with a lead uppercut to opponent's jaw (or body).

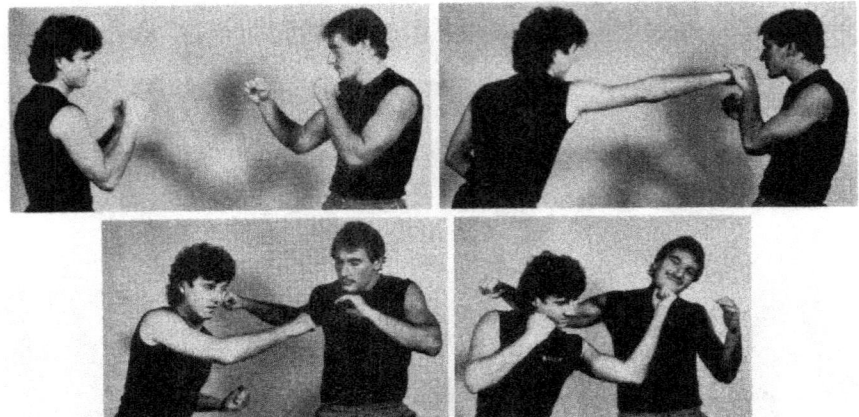

Defender lowers his rear guard while throwing a lead jab, baiting his opponent's lead hook counter, which the defender sidesteps while throwing a rear uppercut to opponent's jaw (or body).

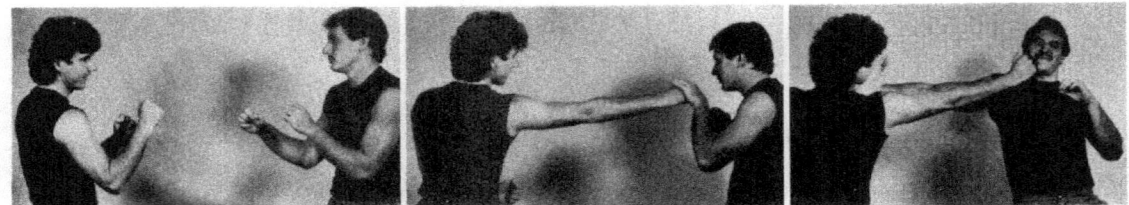

Defender lowers his rear guard while throwing a lead jab, drawing opponent's lead hook counter, which the defender simultaneously parries while scoring with a lead punch.

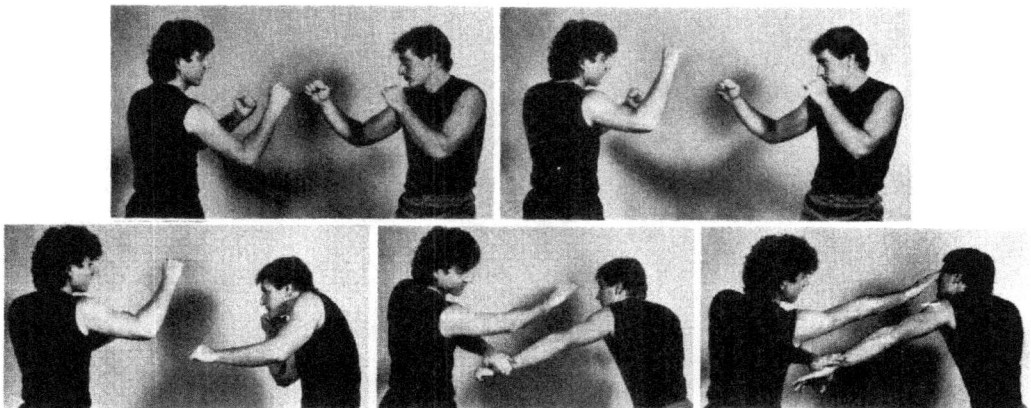

Defender raises lead arm to draw opponent's low rear cross, which he counters with a rear hand parry while simultaneously shooting a finger jab to opponent's eyes.

ATTACK BY DRAWING AGAINST FEET

Defender exposes ribcage to draw opponent's lead hook kick, which he counters by simultaneously parrying the kick while scoring with a rear cross to opponent's face. (Note that defender moves inside the circumference of the kick.)

Defender lowers rear guard to bait opponent's high lead hook kick, which he counters by sidestepping and cutting into opponent's support leg with his own rear hook kick. (Upper body is angulated to avoid kicking leg of opponent.)

Defender exposes body to draw opponent's rear hook kick, which he counters by crashing inside with a lead punch to opponent's face.

One danger in using attack by drawing is that if the opponent suspects he is being baited, he may appear to react to the motion, then counter your attack himself. Therefore it should be used sparingly and judiciously, and should be accompanied by body angulation and a well-covered position in attack.

Used in conjunction with all other ways of attack and with defensive motions, ABD adds variety to your fighting tactics.

KICKBOXING TRAINING DRILLS

Sparring is a matter of choices. Choosing the right weapon to use, finding the correct distance in relation to the opponent, choosing the right moment to attack or defend. Sparring, broken down to its essence, is about timing and distance.

You may have all of the physical tools at your disposal, but if you are not in range to use them, they won't do you any good. Likewise, if you have the tools and the proper distance, but your timing is incorrect, your attack will be less than sure of success.

In learning to kickbox, the initial stage the martial artist concentrates his efforts upon is the development of physical skills. Through constant drilling of precise actions, the fighter conditions his reflexes and reactions to respond immediately to the situation at hand. This conditioning is known as transferring an action from volitional to reflex action—from having to think about it to its becoming reflex. The fighter's choice of action is dependent upon the variety of responses he has conditioned into his neuromuscular system. If he has learned a wide range of reflexive actions, he has a greater choice.

Each physical skill must be learned first, the same way one learns any lesson. But it must be taken beyond that initial level. Automaticity of response is what is desired, where the skill has become second nature to the individual. Then the fighter can concentrate on tactics.

However, "non-thinking" repetition can produce a "robotic" mechanical reaction, rather than relating to the opponent. In training, therefore, quality is to be more valued than simple, non-thinking quantity.

In training with drills, an important point to remember is that both people are learning while drilling. Each training partner must carry out the actions genuinely, remembering that they are assisting each other in developing proper body mechanics, learning proper timing and distance, while increasing the speed at which the drill is being practiced.

To be functional, any sparring should approach reality and approximate combat as closely as possible, which means it must eventually be done at full combat speed. (Techniques with full coordination and increasing speed—precision in all.)

The sparring drills offered in this chapter are only a few of many, and are designed to help a martial artist increase self-confidence while developing a physical skill. Total, unrestricted sparrring is the ultimate choice in Jeet Kune Do.

CATCH DRILLS

The purpose of using a catch against the first punch is to enable you to "gauge the distance" between yourself and the opponent. In all of the following drills you can hit on the first motion if you are able to.

CATCH LEAD JAB—RETURN DRILLS

One man initiates with a high lead jab, partner catches the jab and returns a high lead jab.

One man initiates with a high lead jab, partner catches the jab and returns a low lead jab.

One man initiates with a high lead jab, partner catches the jab and returns a high backfist.

One man initiates with a high lead jab, partner catches the jab and returns a high loose hook.

Closeup of cover

CATCH JAB—
COUNTER REAR CROSS DRILLS

One man initiates a high jab—rear cross combination. Partner catches the jab, catches the cross. (May require backward movement at the same time.)

Defender catches the jab, shoulder rolls away from the rear cross.

Defender catches the jab, uses a shoulder stop against the rear cross. (Usually used against a wide, looping rear cross.)

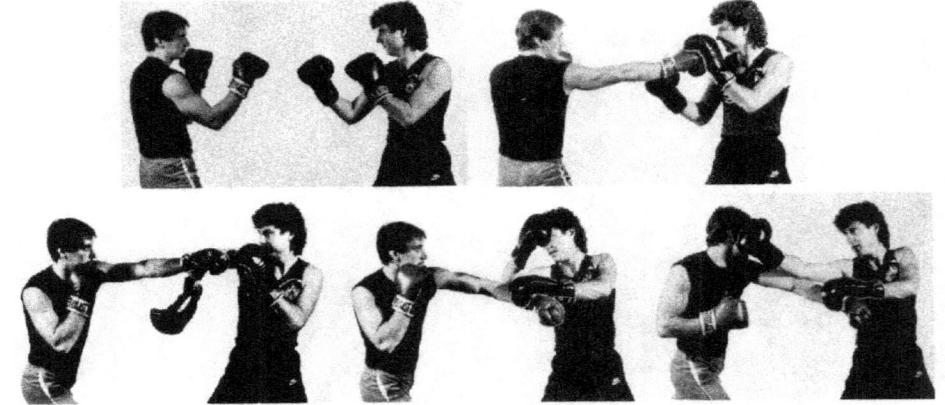

Defender catches the jab, uses a Boang Sao deflection against the rear cross, then traps the opponent's arm and backfists.

Defender catches the jab, slips outside the rear cross and counters to opponent's midsection.

Defender catches the jab, slips inside the rear cross and counters with a low lead jab. (Be aware of opponent's lead hand when on the inside position.)

Defender catches the jab, counters with a lead hook over the opponent's rear cross while shifting backwards. (Good if opponent leans forward with rear cross.)

Defender catches the jab, slips to the outside while countering the cross with a lead uppercut to opponent's jaw. (Usually used against a straight rear cross.)

Defender catches the jab, leans back and side kicks into opponent's knee as rear cross is thrown. (Keep rear hand guard well covered as you kick.)

Defender catches the jab, leans back and hook kicks into opponent's ribs as rear cross is thrown. (Keep rear hand guard high.)

CATCH JAB—
COUNTER LEAD HOOK DRILLS

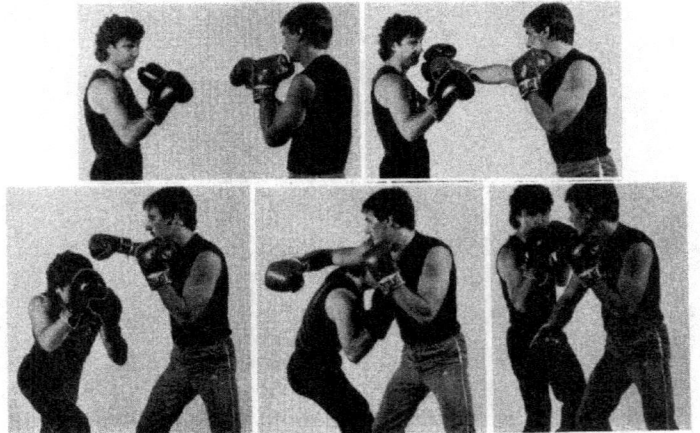

Defender catches the jab, bobs and weaves under the lead hook to the outside of opponent's lead.

Defender catches the jab, shifts inside the circumference of the lead hook while covering with the rear guard hand.

Defender catches the jab, extends rear hand to palm stop into opponent's lead hooking bicep (note high lead hand guard to defend against possible rear hand punch from opponent).

Closeup of palm stop

Defender catches the jab, then sidesteps, angling his body while intercepting opponent's lead hook with a rear cross to opponent's jaw (or body).

CATCH JAB—
COUNTER FRONT UPPERCUT DRILLS

Defender catches the jab, lowers rear forearm to wedge into the crook of opponent's elbow as he attempts a front uppercut.

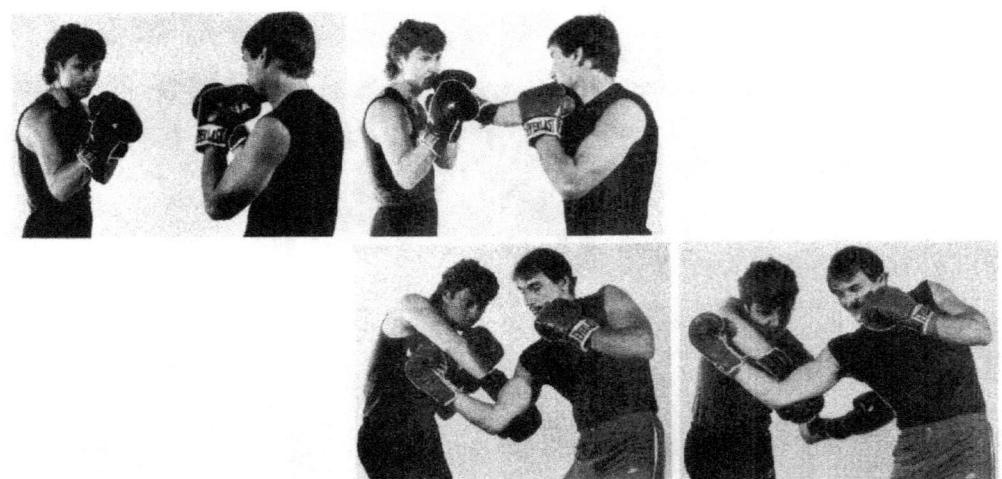

Defender catches the jab, scoops opponent's lead uppercut aside with his lead hand, counters with a shovel hook to opponent's ribs.

Defender catches the jab, shoots his own rear uppercut on top of opponent's lead uppercut, smothering the punch.

Defender catches the jab, angles his body and shoots a rear uppercut under the opponent's uppercut to deflect the blow.

CATCH DRILL VARIATIONS

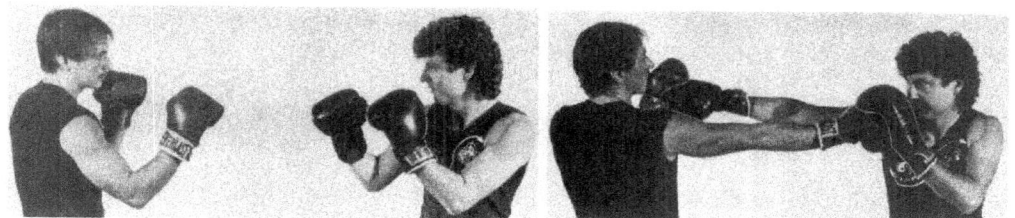

Defender catches the jab and simultaneously returns his own lead jab.

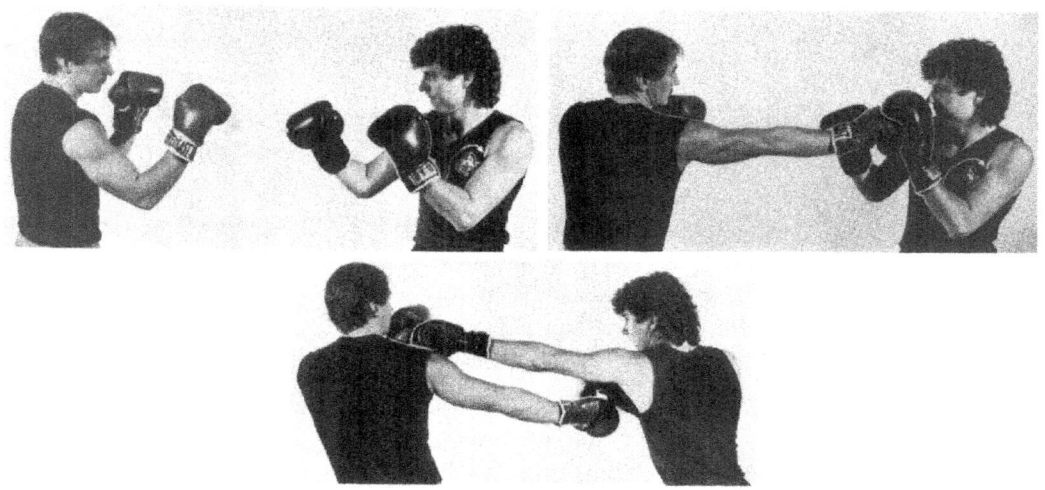

Defender catches the jab, returns a rear cross counter to opponent's jaw.

4 CORNER TRAINING

The following photographs illustrate the basic 4 Corner parries using the rear hand guard.

Front view

Side view

High Outside Gate

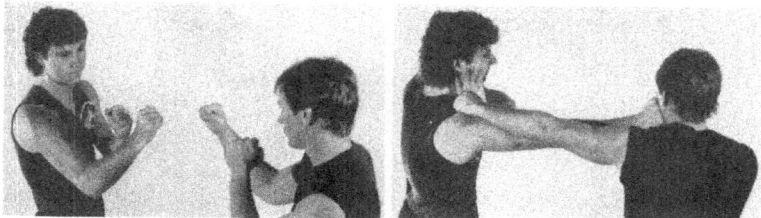

Defender parries opponent's rear cross using a high cross parry (Woang Pak), while simultaneously scoring with a lead punch to opponent's face.

High Inside Gate

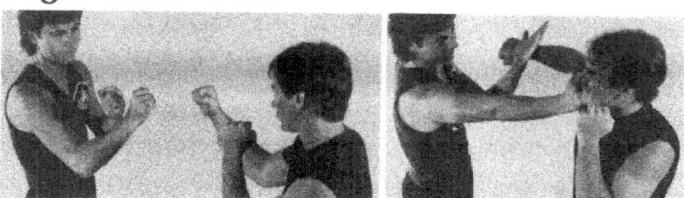

Defender parries opponent's long lead hook using a high inside parry (Tan Sao) while simultaneously countering with a straight lead to opponent's face. (Do not attempt to use this against a tight boxing hook.)

Low Outside Gate

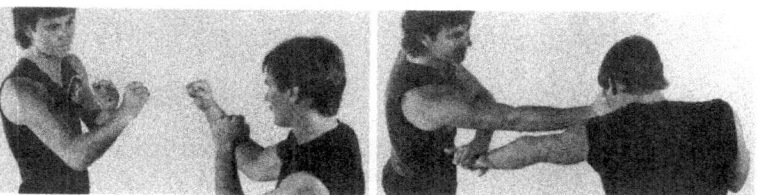

Defender parries opponent's low rear cross using a low outside slapping parry (Ouy Ha Pak) while simultaneously countering with a lead punch to opponent's face.

Low Inside Gate

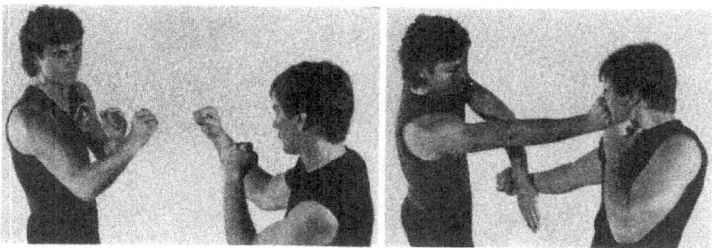

Defender parries a long low hook using a semicircular parry (Loy Ha Pak) and counters simultaneously with a lead punch to opponent's face.

The same 4 corner parries can be done using the lead guard hand.

Front view

Side view

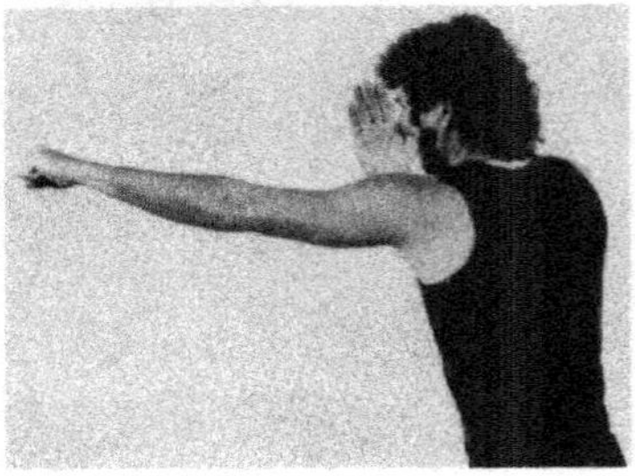

138

4 corner parries can be done three ways:

1. Parry followed by hit.
2. Parry and hit simultaneously.
3. Hit followed by parry.

Possible Angles of Rear Hand Guard for High Inside Parry

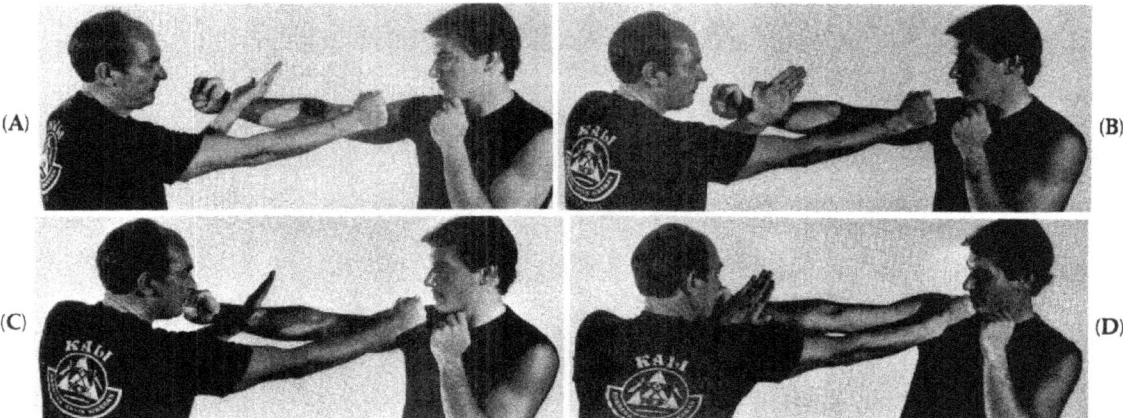

The above photographs illustrate the possible positions that the rear hand may be angled at while using a high inside parry. (**A**) Palm supinated. (**B**) Palm half-supinated. (**C**) Palm pronated. (**D**) Palm half-pronated.

Angles of Fist for Parries

The use of a particular parry is dependent upon which sector a blow is traveling in.

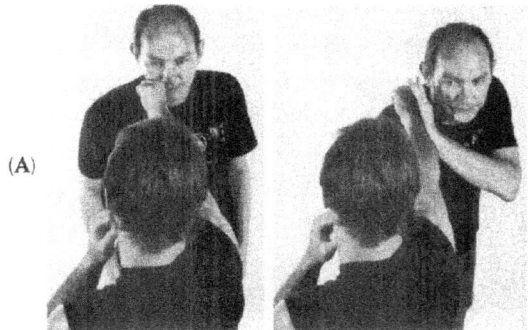

Above photographs illustrate which sector the opponent's punch should be in in order to effectively use a high rear cross parry.

139

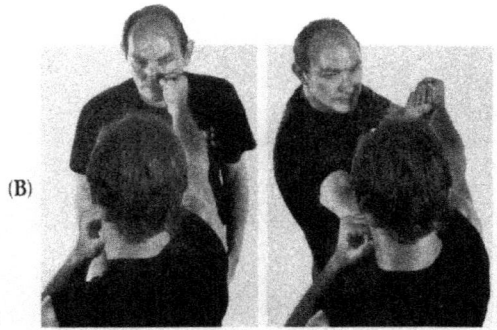

(B)

When the punch is traveling in this sector, one can use a high rear inside parry.

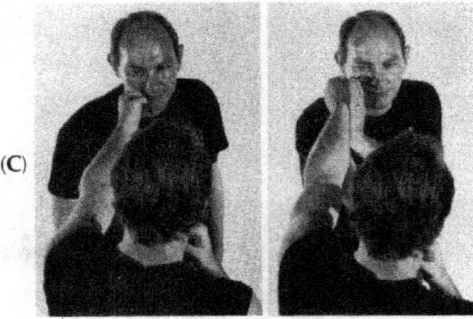

(C)

This time an opponent's rear hand punch is traveling into the same sector as shown in (A), and is parried with the same high rear cross parry.

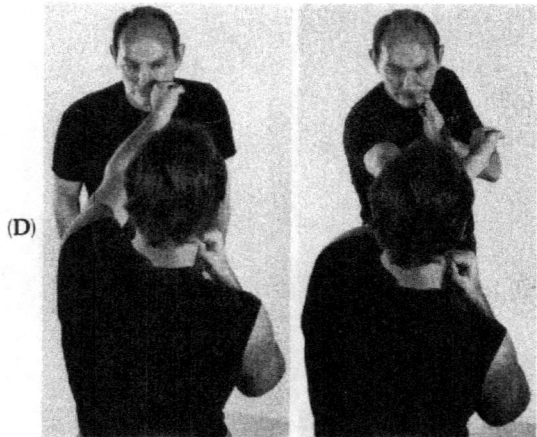

(D)

When the opponent's rear punch is traveling in the same sector as shown in (B), the defender bridges across the punching arm. This is referred to as "cutting into the opponent's tool."

FOOT SPARRING DRILLS
DOUBLE PURSUING HOOK KICK

Partner initiates a step and slide lead hook kick. As opponent shifts out of range while maintaining the same lead, partner closes the distance immediately with a second lead hook kick to score.

LEAD HOOK KICK TO REAR HOOK KICK

This time as partner attempts to close the distance with a step and slide lead hook kick, opponent shifts back out of range and switches leads. Partner plants kicking leg forward and shoots an immediate rear hook kick to opponent.

ANGLING AGAINST LEAD HOOK KICK

As opponent initiates a sliding lead hook kick, partner angles his body away from the kick with a sidestep, and cuts opponent's support leg with a rear hook kick.

ANGLING AGAINST REAR HOOK KICK

As opponent launches a high rear hook kick, partner angles away from the kick using a sidestep, and cuts opponent's support leg with a lead hook kick.

USING A PENDULUM RETREAT AGAINST SIDE KICK—RETURN

As opponent slides in with a side kick, defender pendulum retreats and parries the kick as it reaches full extension, returns a slide lead side kick and closes range.

Same as before only this time the defender returns a slide lead hook kick.

EXCHANGE KICK FOR KICK DRILLS

The purpose of these drills is to parry the opponent's kick and return your own kick as quickly as possible, which he then parries. Usually the drills are practiced in a sequence of either two or three kicks in order to create a rapid-fire exchange.

HOOK KICK EXCHANGE

Opponent initiates with a lead hook kick, which defender parries and immediately returns his own lead hook kick which opponent must parry.

SIDE KICK EXCHANGE

Same as above only this time a side kick is used.

REAR HOOK KICK EXCHANGE

Opponent initiates with a rear hook kick, which the defender parries with a knee raise, and immediately returns his own rear hook kick which opponent must then parry.

COMBINING HANDS AND FEET

As the martial artist progresses and begins to feel comfortable in using his punching and kicking tools, he should begin to combine hands and feet in sparring and drilling, learning how to put combinations together, and developing the ability to shift unconsciously from one to the other as necessary.

TYPES OF OPPONENTS

There are various types of opponents one must learn to deal with. The following sequence of photographs illustrates the different types of opponent one may encounter, and the various distances each type may use.

A Runner

This type of opponent is "flighty" and anytime you try to initiate an attack runs away out of distance of both hands and feet.

One Who Guards With Distance

This opponent uses distance to stay outside of any hand or foot attack, but remains closer than the runner, awaiting an opportunity to score or counter.

One Who Guards and Prepares to Crash (Blocker)

This opponent usually remains well covered and is prepared to block an attack and then counter.

The Jammer

This opponent likes to crash into an attack in order to smother or jam it, and counter. He usually maintains a well-guarded position as he jams.

The Angler

An opponent who likes to use footwork and evasive body angulation to offset an attack.

One can and should learn to deal with every kind of opponent. In this way you will not be surprised by an unfamiliar action.

IN CONCLUSION

The total development of a martial artist is a complex process, for it encompasses so many different aspects. There are physical, mental and emotional differences that all need to be taken into account.

Many people are scared away from certain sports, especially contact sports such as boxing or kickboxing, and generally it is because they have been made to take too many risks too soon. As a result, they feel inadequate, lost, their fears mounting as they feel they are not in control—and eventually they quit.

The solution to this is a process known in sports as "enhancing the safety zone." When a trainer uses this process gradually and professionally, the situation doesn't seem threatening. When dealing with personal risk the martial artist should always be in control of the elements of the activity, for only then can they overcome any fears they may have.

THE CONTINUING ALLURE OF JEET KUNE DO

What continues to draw people to Bruce Lee's martial art of Jeet Kune Do? The reasons are many and varied. For some people it's the cult of celebrity that has been built around Bruce Lee since his untimely passing in 1973. They want to do JKD because that's what Bruce Lee did it and he was just so damn cool. And they believe that if they do it then they'll be cool too. Others have found their inspiration in Bruce Lee's original vision in the late 1960's of creating what he described in letters to his friends as 'the ultimate martial art, or his later belief in the early 1970's of doing away with the idea of styles and systems entirely and his non-restrictive approach to martial art training. Some martial artists are drawn to it because their approach to training is to move from art to art like the person visiting a buffet table who samples bits of many different things. They simply want to taste JKD to see if they like it or not, or to add it (or pieces of it) to the food already on their plate. And there are some who are attracted by Bruce Lee's philosophical credo of personal liberation, both in martial arts and life.

However, for many people the allure is that they see Jeet Kune Do as one of the top brands of martial arts in the world. That's right, you read correctly, "brand." Whether one likes the term or not makes no difference. In the world of martial arts today Jeet Kune Do is recognized as a brand of martial art in the same way such arts as Tai Chi Chuan, Tae Kwon Do, and Hapkido are recognized as established brands of martial art. On March 27, 1981, Jun Fan Gung Fu/Jeet Kune Do was inducted into the Kuo Shu Federation of the Republic of China, making it a legitimate and recognized martial art such as Tai Chi Chuan, etc. It is a recognized 'art', not a 'style.' The term style is inadequate because just as there are various styles and sub-systems within arts such as Tai Chi, Karate, and Jiu Jitsu, there exists within JKD various factions which take different approaches to the teaching and dissemination of the art.

People are drawn to a particular brand because they are inspired by what the brand stands for. It embodies an entire value set that they believe in. For example, Apple is a brand, Harley Davidson is a brand, and Nike is a brand. They're not simply a "brand name", but a brand that people who have a certain mental attitude or who live a certain lifestyle (or who would like to) are drawn to. So yes, JKD is martial art brand. And it's perceived as one of the top brands, not just in the US but around the world. It's a brand those who have a certain mental attitude and/or philosophical bent are drawn to. So what sort of people are those who are drawn towards JKD? I think that for the most part they're creative, free-thinking people who don't need or aren't interested in normal trappings associated with many traditional martial arts such as uniforms and colored belts or sashes. Some of them may be fighters who are more interested in the combative side of the art. Some are interested in learning physical skills they can use if necessary to defend themselves or loved ones should the need arise. And others are interested in developing their self-confidence and/or self-esteem or looking for a philosophy they can use in their approach to life and living. For each of these individuals JKD embodies a value set that they believe in, or would like to believe in:

Personal Liberation (physical, mental, emotional, spiritual) – Jeet Kune Do consists of not only a martial component which has physical discipline and various combative actions as its nucleus, but also a philosophical foundation that underpins the art. People believe JKD can help them cultivate tools and develop the skills they can use to liberate themselves from anything that might hold them back or limit them in any way, be it as a martial artist or a human being.

Totality – Jeet Kune Do is and has always been about the search for martial truth and discovering the roots underlying efficient human movement in combat. Non-fragmented and non-partial, JKD views martial art a unitary 'whole' as opposed to various separated segments (such as only striking or only grappling) and encompasses all the various elements and facets of unarmed combat (striking, grappling, etc.) At the same time, JKD is not about creating a 'melting pot' or a 'mosaic' of different styles, but rather with doing away with the idea of styles entirely. One of Bruce Lee's oft-quoted statements is "If you understand motion, you don't need style."

Freedom – Jeet Kune Do is about total and complete freedom. In his personal notes Bruce Lee defined martial as "an unrestricted athletic expression of an individual soul." JKD, at its core, believes the individual is more important than any style or system. The most fundamental principle of JKD is that, as a living and creative individual, a martial artist should not be bound by a prescribed set of rules or techniques, and should be free to explore and expand, and have the freedom to experiment and innovate various techniques and body movements to discover their own potential and find out what works best for themselves individually – to find their own way rather than relying on someone else's. In combat a JKD practitioner is free to use technique or dispense with it as they see fit and according to the dictates of a particular situation -- they're not locked in or bound to using only one way or only certain techniques.

The martial arts world today is a totally different place from where it was during Bruce Lee's lifetime. The martial art audience changes as time goes on, and their desires and demands change and may be very different than those who preceded them.

JKD's place in it may be different than it was when it first burst onto the martial art scene, but it retains its position as one of the top martial art brands in the world. The core values, the things JKD stands for and aspires to remain constant. Those things have never changed (nor should they). And that's why countless people continue to be drawn to it. That is the continuing allure of Jeet Kune Do.

HOW TO MAKE BRUCE LEE'S NOTES WORK FOR YOU

In his never-ending quest for personal development, Bruce Lee went to incredible lengths to gain insight and learning that would aid him in actualizing his full potential, drawing from all forms of combative arts, modern dance, bodybuilding, exercise physiology, kinesiology, philosophy and psychology. And in the years before copy machines, computers, printers, and digital media recording devices were part of everyone's daily life, Lee put pen (or sometimes pencil) to paper and recorded his thoughts, observations, and ideas on these as well as other subjects, leaving behind thousands of pages of written and typed notes. Many of these notes have been compiled into books over the years since his passing.

We're not going to get into any form of discussion here regarding where many of these notes may have originated or come from, whether they were his original thoughts or drawn from another source. We will leave that up to others. Regardless of their origins, if you truly desire to get the most out of Jeet Kune Do it is essential to know how to make Bruce Lee's notes work for you; how to bring them to life for yourself and use them to assist you to achieve your fullest potential as a martial artist.

Lee's notes have been likened to guideposts, or clues, that can lead an individual to their highest level of self-expression as a martial artist. But guideposts and clues do a person little or no good if they don't know how to read or interpret them correctly.

The first thing one needs to understand is how to approach and study the notes. When reading Bruce Lee's notes, three intrinsic principles should guide your study. These principles may, in the beginning, require several separate readings but in time can be done concurrently. The three principles are:

Understand the notes: You need to comprehend thoroughly and perceive clearly the nature of what you're reading. What are the particular writings or notes you are studying saying?

Interpret the notes: To "interpret" means, "to bring out or explain the meaning of something." In other words, what do the notes you're studying mean? What is it relating to? Many times, people immediately rush to the application stage of Lee's teachings and bypass the theoretical stage. They want to know what a technique or principle means to them before they understand what Lee intended it to mean.

Evaluate the notes: To evaluating something means to judge or determine its worth or quality. In other words, is the given principle, technique, or action right or wrong for them? Is it valid or not? Unfortunately, a lot of people tend to skip over the first two principles and jump right into evaluating Lee's notes. They judge a particular principle or concept to be right or wrong before they understand what it says or before they interpret its meaning.

The preceding three intrinsic principles are, however, by themselves, inadequate, because they're only one half of the equation. To study Bruce Lee's notes successfully and get the most out of them, one also needs three important extrinsic aids:

Experience: Experience is the only way to interpret and relate what has been read. A person who has little or no experience in martial arts and/or philosophy is going to be at a distinct disadvantage in understanding, interpreting, and evaluating Lee's notes. By way of example, while I may be able to tell you what I like or don't like about a particular painting by a master like Van Gogh, I will not be able to interpret and evaluate the painting in the same way as a person who has and education and background in fine arts. However, experience by itself is not enough. One needs to research their experience. Experience that has been understood and reflected upon informs and enlightens your study.

Other Books, Writings and Materials: Books and writings and other material such as various types of digital media that precede or advance the subject you're studying can be very significant. Oftentimes books or notes can have greater meaning when they're read in relation to other writings. I've had the privilege of perusing the books in Bruce Lee's personal library at great length on numerous occasions. At the same time, I've also established my own library that includes books on martial arts, Western fencing, physical fitness, kinesiology, philosophy, psychology, and various other categories of interest. Studying and analyzing these books has unquestionably helped to increase my understanding of Lee's notes. Bruce Lee always approached a subject wanting to know as much as possible about it and with an open mind ready to absorb new information. If he were alive today, there's no doubt that he would avail himself of all sources of information including books, videos, films, dvds, and the internet to gain access to the most up-to--date information on whatever subject that interested him or that he was studying. And you should do the same thing.

Live discussion: The final extrinsic aid is live discussion, which means the interaction that occurs among individuals as they pursue a particular course of action. I've spent countless hours discussing Bruce's notes regarding various aspects of JKD with my close friends Cass Magda, John Little, and Linda Lee Cadwell, sometimes just between the two of us, and other times with other friends, colleagues, and/or students. When you discuss and debate certain issues, techniques, or philosophical attitudes relating to JKD, many times new insights emerge that might have never occurred without this type of exchange.

As important as it is to successfully research Lee's notes, it's equally important to know how to use them. The first step of this process is to read the notes without trying to fit them into established categories. The goal here is to simply grasp the content of the material, the essence of what's being presented, and to understand it. Expect to hear new things in new ways when you read the notes at different times and don't be concerned if you don't get some things in the first reading. It might take several readings before you fully comprehend something. All of us have had the "ah-ha!" experience of reading something over and over and then, suddenly understanding what it means. Such a "Wow, now I get it!" experience of understanding oftentimes catapults you into onto a new level of growth and freedom. To assist with this, you might find it useful each time you read the notes to use a differently colored pen to mark certain things that stand out to you at that time. Another idea is to keep a journal or notebook handy to jot down thoughts and impressions that occur to you while reading.

The next step is to investigate why Lee drew a particular essence from an art or why he chose to absorb something into his own art. Ask yourself questions such as, "What is it about this particular technique that Bruce Lee felt was useful or valid to what he was doing?" Analyze it by breaking it down

into its component parts and examining it to find out its interrelationship with other material in Lee's notes.

The third step is to apply what you are studying. Theory without application means nothing. You've got to take the material you're investigating onto the floor and test it and see if, and how well it works under pressure and in realistic situations. Keep in mind, though, that just because you may not be able to do it or use it at that moment doesn't mean that it's not valid or that it's no good.

The final step is to evaluate the material, to judge the value of it for a given purpose. Ask yourself, "Is this particular principle or technique valid or not? How does it relate to me? Does it have application to what I'm doing?" If, for example, the style of martial art you practice doesn't believe in the use of any type of hand immobilization attacks, then sensitivity training exercises such as chi sao may have no application for you. At the same time, keep in mind that just because something might not have an application for you, that doesn't mean it won't have an application for someone else.
The following are some pitfalls you should try to avoid when studying and/or using Bruce Lee's notes:

- Simply memorizing and regurgitating Lee's words, ideas, etc. Anybody can repeat someone else's words by rote. The important thing is not how much fixed knowledge or information you've accumulated, it's what you can use and apply that counts.

- Taking the material in Bruce Lee's notes to be the "Bible" or gospel of martial arts. Some people approach JKD very dogmatically and with the fundamentalist view that "If it's not in the Tao of JKD, or if it's not in Bruce's writings, then it's not JKD." This is the very antithesis of Lee's teachings. The things Bruce Lee wrote down are not true because he wrote them down, he wrote them down because he found them to be true. To him, each thing he wrote down represented a truth, not the truth. No one has a monopoly on truth. There is no "one way."

- Thinking that Bruce Lee's notes are all there is to his way of martial arts.

- Adding your own interpretation to Bruce Lee's material. Understand that I'm not saying that you shouldn't interpret Lee's material. I am simply reminding you to keep things in proper context. Oftentimes people read something with an eye towards finding support for what they themselves are

doing (this is known as "confirmation bias"). For example, in Lee's notes it states, "Investigate into fighting from the ground…develop such mastery that one can fight safely from the ground." But Lee doesn't make a point of telling you to study any specific style of ground-fighting or martial art that includes ground-fighting. The point is to hear what Bruce Lee is saying, not what we want him to say.

- Concretizing or solidifying Bruce Lee's guideposts into laws. Bruce changed his mind about publishing his notes when he came to the realization that trying to encapsulate fighting into words was like trying to capture something on paper that is alive and constantly changing. It was, he concluded, "like attempting to tie a pound of water into a manageable shape." Don't calcify what should remain alive and growing.

- Starting from a conclusion. Remember, to taste someone else's tea you must first empty your cup of preconceived ideas, notions, etc. Begin with an open mind, a blank slate if you will.

Bruce Lee's notes are in some ways an extension of Bruce himself. They describe the direction of his studies and shed light on his own process of intellectual growth and development as a martial artist. As such, they can serve as a direct pipeline to his way of thinking, feeling, and researching. Bruce's notes can also act as a navigational guide, like a compass, which can help direct you towards where you want to be as a martial artist. If you know how to use a compass, even if the terrain changes, a road becomes blocked, or a detour arises, you can remain on course toward your ultimate destination. To do that, however, you must know where it is that you want to go. Once you know that, then you can take all of the information in Lee's notes and consider it; debate it, turn it upside down; look at it from your own perspective; refine it to suit you; rearrange it; keep what you think will work for you; and even throw some of it out (just make sure you know why you're throwing it out).

One final piece of advice. Don't allow anyone to simply hand you the truth. Take an experiential attitude and find out for yourself what works for you. See Bruce Lee's notes as a literary work in progress, not as something that was finished or completed. Remember, "If you understand it and can use it, it belongs to no one; it's yours."

JEET KUNE DO: GUIDE TO EQUIPMENT TRAINING
By Chris Kent

"MAXIMIZE YOUR FIGHTING SKILLS"
Regardless of what styles or methods of martial arts you train in, "Jeet Kune Do: Guide to Equipment Training" offers comprehensive and cohesive training information that will help you maximize your combat skills and achieve your full potential as a martial artist and fighter. Detailed and progressive instruction on how to use the heavy bag, focus mitts, forearm pad, kicking shield, etc... makes this book the main source of information about the proper use of equipment training. This book will take you to a new level of integration and mastery of your art, regardless of the style, if what you are interested in is real contact power!

US $45.00 – 7 x 10 – 350 pages approx.

FOR PURCHASE VISIT:
WWW. MARTIALARTSDIGITAL.COM

ENCYCLOPEDIA OF JEET KUNE DO - A to Z
By Chris Kent

Jeet Kune Do is the art of expressing the human body in combative form. It is not a "style" or "system" of martial art as conventionally defined. Nor is it simply an eclectic conglomeration of fighting techniques from various arts combined with philosophical dogma that is convenient. Jeet Kune Do is a rational, well thought-out approach to "total" martial art training.
The "Encyclopedia of Jeet Kune Do" is designed to serve as a resource guide, not only for the person training in Jeet Kune Do, but for any martial artist sincerely interested in enhancing his or her performance and achieving one's full potential.
Many of the principles and training methods illustrated in one section or chapter of this book can and should be cross-referenced with motions or actions in another. The goal is for you, the reader, to use this book to improve your understanding and working knowledge of the art, science, and philosophy of unarmed combat known as Jeet Kune Do. Remember, it's not how much you absorb, but how much of what you've absorbed that you can apply "alively" that counts.

US $34.95 – 7 x 10 – 350 pages approx.

FOR PURCHASE VISIT:
WWW. MARTIALARTSDIGITAL.COM

ESSENTIAL JEET KUNE DO
The Way of Intercepting Fist
By Tim Tackett

This book will serve way to decide what will work the best for you and what aspects of JKD you need to keep, as well as throw away. I feel that it would be impossible to learn this from your instructor, as he will mainly focus on what works best for him. I have been fortunate to have learned from many of the senior students of Bruce Lee and have noticed that they all focus on certain things and not on what some the others are doing. For some it may be the boxing aspects. For some it may be footwork. For others it was trapping energy and the Wing Chun elements. It was only when we started focusing on the Western fencing aspects of JKD that I was able to understand and focus on what has become my essence of JKD. Of course, an instructor cannot just hand you what will become your essence or foundation of your own JKD. This is something that you must discover for yourself as you work to become more a more efficient JKD practitioner. The purpose of this book is too show you most of what we teach in my garage and the basic principles behind each. Once you have worked on these you will come to realize what will work for you and what will not. Some of you will want to focus on distance and footwork. Others will feel comfortable crashing the line. Whatever works for you is the main thing. Just use the book as guideline to discover your own essential JKD.

US $45.00 – 7 x 10 – 350 pages approx.

FOR PURCHASE VISIT:
WWW. MARTIALARTSDIGITAL.COM

JEET KUNE DO PRINCIPLES
For All Martial Artist
By Tim Tackett

The title of this book is "Jeet Kune Do Principles". Principles and concepts that ALL Martial Artists – regardless of style - can use in their daily training. In fact, most of these principles are used everyday by all martial artists around the world, and most like speed and timing, are not unique to the art of Jeet Kune Do. The purpose of this book is to explain some of these principles and share some ideas on how to train for them. Some are principles like the use of distance and broken rhythm in combat, while others are sayings on combat by the founder of JKD Bruce Lee that perfectly illustrate a principle or a fighting idea. To understand the root, you need to understand the principles.
The principles of Jeet Kune Do are universal, but unfortunately these principles are no longer stressed as much anymore, because there is too much focus on "technique" alone, and seeing how many techniques you can "add" to your toolbox.
The purpose of this work is to discuss some of the principles that the art of JKD focuses on, and to give you some examples to put those principles in action. The hope of this book is that you do the same with the main techniques you either are studying or teaching – regardless of your style.

US $45.00 – 7 x 10 – 350 pages approx.

FOR PURCHASE VISIT:
WWW. MARTIALARTSDIGITAL.COM

www.ingramcontent.com/pod-product-compliance
Lightning Source LLC
Chambersburg PA
CBHW080736230426
43665CB00020B/2763